Greater Expectations

Greater Expectations

A SOURCE BOOK FOR WORKING WITH GIRLS AND YOUNG WOMEN

TRICIA SZIROM AND SUE DYSON

British Edition edited by Hazel Slavin

Learning Development Aids

LDA

Learning Development Aids
Duke Street
Wisbech
Cambs. PE13 2AE
England

© Living and Learning (Cambridge) Ltd. 1986
© In Australia and New Zealand: YWCA of Australia
© Original Text: Tricia Szirom and Sue Dyson
© Illustrations: Linda Combi

First printed 1986
Reprinted 1987
Second Reprint 1988

ISBN 0 905 114 19 1

Printed in England by
Ebenezer Baylis & Son Ltd
The Trinity Press, Worcester and London

CONTENTS

Acknowledgements

Many people have influenced us in writing this book. The contributions made by co-workers and people in groups with whom we have worked, as well as friends and mentors, are appreciated by us, and if we forget to mention your name, well, we never said we were perfect!

Some people we would like to especially thank for their contributions and ideas are Mary-Ruth Marshall and Sue Morely. We would also like to thank the participants at the Avalon Workshop 1983 for helping us test the strategies and ideas in this book:

Jenni, Jill, Kathy, Vivienne, Jane, Merryn, Mexie, Wendy, Isabelle, Trish, Dorothy, Mandy, Bev, Karen, Sally, Robyn, Jonny, Meredith, Lynne, Mary, Brigitte, Hima, Pamela and Hope.

For their support, criticism, influence and patience, we thank Shirley Sampson, Wendy Rose and Bess Carr, Rosemary Craig and Elise Carter. For their love and support, we thank The Clarity Collective, and for her love, constructive criticism, relevant questions and many cups of tea, Jenny Cameron.

We would like to thank the following for their strategies:
Mary-Ruth Marshall, 'This is my best friend' (p.45), 'My body — body image' (p.141), 'A relationship must be . . .' (p.177); Sue Morley, 'Herstory' (p.70); Sidney Simon, 'Random words' (p.88); Colleen Vale and Linda Naughton, 'Hands off' (p.154).

This book was made possible with the help of a grant from the Australian Department of Education and Youth Affairs.

Dedication

This book is dedicated to the women in our lives: our mothers, friends, sisters and colleagues who have loved us, cared for us, supported us and challenged us to greater expectations.

Foreword to the British Edition

I have tried to ensure that this edition of Greater Expectations remains faithful to the original Australian book in both its concept and content. It starts with the premise that growing up as a girl is not easy and that although we have made great progress in equal opportunities in schools, colleges and youth clubs, girls are still disadvantaged.

One way of helping girls to be more powerful and able to take control of their lives is by positive teaching programmes designed to raise self esteem and awareness and practice assertive skills. This book offers a series of strategies and games to help that process. Many of the strategies have been re-written for the British edition and reflect our multi-cultural society. Although the games and projects are designed for use with young women, many of them are easily adapted for use with women's groups of all ages.

The support and influence of many women friends have helped shape my ideas but I would like to thank Naomi Pfeffer and Dot Griffiths for thoughtful suggestions and Jennie Popay for her re-writing of the women and employment workshops. Hannah MacIlwaine remained constantly supportive and interested in the project and was helpful and painstaking in checking corrections and alterations.

Hazel Slavin

Being a Girl Isn't Always Easy

Introduction

It is a well-established and documented fact that women in Britain are disadvantaged in every way, in comparison to men. The reasons for these disadvantages are many and complex, but they can all be described in terms of structural or systematic sexism. That is to say, the system under which we operate, the social, cultural, economic and political structures, are designed to exclude women, or to discriminate against them as a group.

This is not altogether surprising if we examine history and the way in which the system originated. In the mid-twentieth century, however, we are learning at one level to have different expectations of life. One of the most powerful messages about living in a Western society is that it claims equality to be both essential and attainable for all people.

Girls and women learn this at one level, while at another, from experience and observation, they learn that they are definitely not equal. No wonder many women feel confused and in conflict about their role in society. In this context, women are questioning both their personal relationships and the structures which have remained unchanged for centuries.

Some areas where women experience their lack of equality are in employment and education. Women are more likely than men to be unemployed. They constitute the majority of the hidden unemployed, those people who have become so disillusioned about the prospect of finding work that they do not register with Job Centres. Therefore they do not show up in the statistics collected by the Government. Women derive fewer benefits from their level of success in schooling than do comparably educated males. Overall, women are assigned a lower status, shown up by their inability to command equal incomes with men, and their under-representation in decision making structures.

In our society, minority groups experience extreme discrimination. Women in minority groups are usually doubly disadvantaged. Oppression as women is compounded by such factors as race, ethnic origins, class, sexual preference and disability.

The handicaps engendered for women by structural sexism often mean that the range of options open to women are limited. Studies have shown that girls and young women, when asked to describe their future life, cannot see beyond their mid-twenties.

Typically, a young woman will describe a future where she finishes school, works for a few years, marries, has children and lives 'happily ever after'. This is simply not the reality for most women today. Many are destined to work to contribute to family incomes or become single parents; others never marry and are responsible for their own support. Women today need to keep their options open. They are more likely to be unemployed than men, but they share similar responsibilities and have the same need to earn an income.

Many women find that they have limited their options by subject choice at school, and in post-school education and training. They enter an area of employment with limited opportunities, and find themselves locked into work which is either boring or rapidly disappearing due to technological change.

In order to develop a wider range of choices and to broaden the options available, it is important for women to learn to understand the structures and context which contribute to their lack of equality, and to develop skills to deal with, or change, their situation. There is also a need to ensure that opportunities are provided in areas like education and employment for women to gain equality of access. Positive discrimination programmes are one way of achieving this, equal opportunity programmes are another. Both have the effect of empowering women.

Experience has shown that some of the most effective ways of working towards personal and social change for women is to work together in women-only groups, with the positive support of other women who share similar aims. In this way, women increase their awareness about attitudes and issues, while developing confidence and positive feelings of self esteem.

There are many courses and programmes offered for women that claim to give them power over their lives. What is different about the kind of course that can be run using this book, is that it works at more than one level. This is demonstrated by the framework upon which this book is based.

The framework

Socialization is a complex process which involves a range of forces. It is the process through which individuals learn the values, expectations and rules of their society. These, in turn, have a powerful influence over the way people see and feel about themselves as individuals, and as females or males. The term *self esteem* is used to describe the way a person feels about her or himself, and *self concept* is used to describe how a person consciously views her or himself.

It is well established that women have lower, or less positive, self esteem than men. Positive self esteem is important if we are to develop the knowledge, skills and attitudes that will help us work towards developing our full potential as human beings. In many ways, self esteem is the filter through which we view the world. How we see ourselves enhances or hampers our ability to cope with or change the environment.

The kinds of socializing agents discussed in this book include language, the family, sex role stereotyping, the media and sexual harassment. These are only a few of the complex and many forces surrounding us. Socialization is a dynamic process and whilst acknowledging the complexity of this process, it is important to remember that we are not totally passive recipients. How we respond to the messages about society's rules and expectations in turn influences these rules and expectations. Because of the power and subtlety of socialization, the response of any one person will probably have a limited impact. However, change is possible and by working together in groups women have proved that they can break down the barriers imposed and change the rules.

People are constantly making decisions about themselves, their lives and their environment. Even waiting to see what will happen is a form of decision — not to decide is to decide. There are a range of *decision making* approaches. The one we use in this book includes making it possible for people to examine what might be important to them; helping them make clear in their own minds the options and choices available or desirable; listening with interest to their ideas and thinking; providing information when appropriate; and perhaps creating some discomfort or dissonance when people handicap themselves by limiting their choices. This latter may be most important in the case of girls and young women. Sex role conditioning limits choices. Social stereotypes — for instance, women are intuitive and men are logical — almost always vest power in males, e.g. the power to make decisions. Power is about more than simply limiting choices: it is about restricting choice.

One of the startling pieces of information to come out of research into creative and cognitive thinking, is that while girls have the ability to make choices which reflect life priorities they consciously or subconsciously diminish the use of this skill from the middle teen years onwards. Evidence suggests that girls have a capacity for this skill to a greater degree than boys.

The issues about which we make decisions relate to our health, education, employment and lifestyle. These are at both a personal and a political level. The decisions we make and how we make them can have an effect on the external factors and on the person who makes them. The results of our decisions are constantly with us, and our knowledge, attitudes and skills are shaped by these results, for better or for worse.

The *context* in which we make decisions, the social, cultural, economic and political structures in which we live, affects the decisions we make, and also how we make them. These structures are transmitted through the socialization process. The range of options and choices available are dictated by these structures, and can be expressed as *power*. This power is, in our society, mostly oppressive to women; only through the process of *empowerment* can women hope to gain equality.

The activities in this book address the three inter-related areas of knowledge, attitudes and skills; they are esteem building and designed to lead to the empowerment of women. *Knowledge* includes the information and facts necessary to make decisions and to give us access to options. *Skills* in communication, assertiveness, relationships, conflict resolution and negotiating, provide the means for effective use of knowledge. Understanding ourselves and being clear about our *values* and *attitudes* further enhances our skills, especially those of decision making and priority setting. These three areas are interlinked, none exist in isolation, and each influences the other.

Before You Even Start

Working with the group
Establishing the need for women-only groups

In establishing programmes for women and working with girl-only groups, you will be confronted by your own sexism and prejudices, and those of the people around you. Here are some of the most used arguments against developing special programmes for young women.

- It is sexist because boys are excluded.
- Increasing women's skills and knowledge makes them dissatisfied and can even break up the family.
- Young women need to deal with reality and having them in a single sex group does not force them to do so.
- Boys have problems and also need groups.
- As we already have equal opportunity and equal pay no more change is needed.

At a personal level you may be accused of being a man-hater and aggressive.

There are, however, very good reasons for conducting women-only groups and well documented evidence and research to back them up.

- Women are discriminated against in every sphere of their lives including employment, health, education and recreation.
- Socialization for females and males is different. The outcome of this is that women often lack self confidence, self esteem and life management skills.
- Women are taught to defer to men in all situations including discussion groups and education programmes. Women behave differently in single sex groups than they do in mixed groups.
- In mixed groups men control the conversation. In women-only groups, women have all of the time and space available, including the opportunity to take on leadership functions which are usually denied to them in mixed groups.

- In single sex groups women are more likely to deal with their central issues and concerns, whereas in mixed groups men set the agenda.
- Most of the problems and concerns that women want to deal with have developed in mixed sex environments such as the family, schools and workplaces. The problems develop because women are discriminated against in all of these situations. Providing them with a setting which removes that discrimination and affirms their experiences, allows them to work in new ways which can then be applied in other situations.

During the 1950s and 1960s, large numbers of women began to reject the notion that their dissatisfaction was a result of their own inadequacy. As they shared their experience they discovered that they were not alone in their analysis of the world and their place within it. The consciousness raising groups of the 1960s and 1970s provided individual women with an opportunity to share their experience, and gain knowledge and skills which led them to identify many of their common personal experiences as political. They also provided women with the support necessary to make changes both within their own lives and the society around them.

Developing community support

As change does not occur in a vacuum, it is important to take into account the environment in which the group will function. Many of the strategies suggested in this book depend on co-operation from community agencies and services. It is essential to develop support before starting the course. Although the specific agencies will differ from one community to another, the groundwork remains the same. Many agencies which work with, or provide services to, young people, focus attention on the needs and interests of young men and may not have considered that young women's needs are different. Some of them may need convincing that affirmative action is necessary for young women.

Prepare yourself

As part of making contact with other agencies and services, collect information on the situation of young women in your community.

The information you collect should include:

- the current services and programmes for young people in the community and the percentage of young women involved in those programmes;
- the specific health needs of young women and the services available for them;
- the number of unplanned pregnancies and the number of single mothers;
- the unemployment rates for young women as a percentage of youth unemployment, and the jobs available for young women;
- the number of female early school leavers and the estimated number of young women who are part of the hidden unemployed.

Gaining support for any new innovative programme can be time consuming but it is worth the effort and essential to its long term success. If you involve young women and members of your agency, they will be more likely to give support later on.

Contacting the group

While the strategies in this book can be used by individuals or with large groups, we recommend a maximum of 20 and a minimum of 12 per group.

If you are not working with an already established group, you may want to bring together a group for the course. This can be done by radio and newspaper advertisements, posters and brochures, or personal contact.

Radio and newspaper publicity Prepare a concise, clearly written statement, in the words you would like to have used in announcements and take it personally to a local radio station or local newspaper. These kind of announcements are often free. The media usually respond well to prepared material and can be a good venue for publicity.

Brochures Be sure to have an easy-to-read brochure that states all the necessary information. It can be hand-written or typed, as long as it is clear and easy to understand. It will be more eye-catching if decorated with an appropriate picture or graphic. Include:

- the name of the course;
- the nature of the course, its aims and objectives, what it offers participants;
- all relevant times, dates, address and phone numbers;
- who is organising the group;
- who will be working with the group and what qualifies them to do this;
- the costs involved;
- who the course is for.

If you have not had previous experience in preparing press releases and brochures, it can be useful to seek the advice of someone who is experienced in this field. Most people are happy to share their knowledge and expertise.

Planning and evaluating a course

The planning process is the same whether it is for a single strategy, a session or a course. An effective plan will be logical, sequential, realistic and consistent with the needs and interests of the participants and, if appropriate, to the aims of the sponsoring agency. It is useful to have a flexible plan for the entire course as well as a specific plan for each session. When planning the overall course, ask yourself the following questions:

Why is this course being run? Set clear objectives for the course. What will be achieved by the end? The objectives should be appropriate to the learning needs and expectations of the participants.

Where will the course be held? Whether you are working with an already established group or starting work with a new one, the venue is extremely important. You will need a venue that:

- is accessible to transport;
- offers privacy and can be used without interruptions;
- has a comfortable room temperature;
- provides facilities for making tea and coffee;
- has comfortable seating for all members of the group;
- is well lit;
- has space for the activities which require small group work and movement, but is not so large that the group feels lost;
- preferably has carpet or rugs so that participants can sometimes work on the floor;
- can have posters or flipcharts displayed;
- has moveable furniture so that activities can be conducted.

Take time to find a suitable venue and, if appropriate, involve members of the group in the selection so that they feel comfortable with it.

Who will be involved in the course? This question relates to the participants, resource personnel and workers. In many cases the programme will be developed for an already established group, but if this is not the case it is important to consider the individuals who will be involved. The resource personnel should be appropriate to the needs and interests of the group and not involved just because they are there and may have something interesting to say. In women-only groups it is important to use women workers and resource personnel as they provide valuable role models.

When will the course be run? What time of the year, week, and day will be most appropriate for the course? In some situations you will not have a choice. It is important, however, to consider the needs, interests and other commitments of the participants. for example, if the majority of the group are undertaking school exams, it is best to avoid exam time.

How? This question covers a wide range of hows such as: how will participants be contacted? how will I handle unforeseen situations? how will the objectives be achieved?

Having clearly defined course and session objectives will help answer these questions. Knowing what you want the outcome of a session or course to be makes it easier to select strategies that will achieve this.

When choosing a strategy, ask yourself how it will achieve the objectives. Differentiate between process (what will happen within the group), and content (what the group will learn). For example, increasing communication within the group is a process objective, while learning about women's role in the workforce is a content objective. Remember that strategies are a means to an end, and not an end in themselves. Understand the strategy before you use it. Learn the rules and be aware of any pitfalls. Practice the instructions out loud. Be flexible and change the strategy if necessary. Stay involved even if you've done the strategy many times before.

What equipment and resources are needed? It is essential to ask this question before the course commences and then prior to each session. Any equipment should be set up and tested before the session. Also check that you have the necessary equipment such as copies of work sheets, pens and flipcharts that are required for a strategy.

Once you have answered these questions use the course planner (p. 10) to develop flexible plans; this will provide an overall framework which can be adapted as the group develops

Course planner

The course aims are:

Venue:

Dates and times:

Date (when)	Session No.	Objectives (why)	Activity or Strategy (how)	Resource Personnel (who)	Equipment and Resources (what)

Session planner

When you have completed the Course Planner, you will have an overall flexible plan. Each session will also need to be planned. This can be done between sessions so that the group have maximum input into the course and are involved in setting directions for themselves.

The following is an example of a session planner.

Objective:
By the end of this session participants will have identified a range of women's health issues and will have discussed the different health expectations for females and males.

Time Activity or Strategy	Equipment	Person responsible
7.00pm This is my best friend (p.45)	16 copies of the worksheet	Sue
7.30pm Women's health brainstorm (p.132)	Flipchart paper & felt tip pens	Jenny
7.50pm Coffee break		
8.00pm To be healthy (p.136)	16 copies of the worksheet	Sue
8.45pm Evaluation voting (p.34)	None	Jenny
9.00pm Finish		

Evaluation against objectives:

- involvement in the brainstorm will identify a range of women's health issues;
- *To be healthy* will provide a stimulus for discussing the different health expectations;
- *Evaluation voting* will indicate participants' reaction to and involvement in the session.

Note:
The activities and strategies should be used in any order depending upon the needs of the group.

Self directed learning

Self directed learning describes a process through which individuals take the initiative for identifying their learning needs, formulating goals, identifying resources, choosing and putting into practice appropriate learning strategies and evaluating the outcome. Most people have only experienced learning situations in which they are expected to be passive recipients of knowledge. Group members may not be prepared for a course which uses a self directed learning approach and, initially, will need encouragement to take responsibility for their own learning.

To a greater or lesser extent, all of the strategies in this book are based on the principles of self directed learning. When planning the course begin with strategies that match the current abilities of the group and gradually work towards the strategies that require total group and individual control.

Evaluation

Evaluation is the means by which you assess how effective you have been, the direction in which the group is moving, the appropriateness of your leadership style and the relevance of the course content. At an individual level, evaluation can enable participants to assess their own learning and the personal value of the course.

Evaluation is also an important part of the planning process as the evaluation from one session can assist in the planning of future sessions. Evaluation can also be used as part of the accountability process for the course.

Listed below are some useful questions to ask when evaluating a session. These have been divided into three major headings:

Group Process Was there co-operation and mutual support? Do all members feel a sense of belonging? Did everyone enjoy the opportunity to contribute and try new things? Did the session run smoothly? Are trust and support being maintained in the group? Are the process objectives being achieved?

Content Were the activities and strategies appropriate to the group? Was the content covered? Was there enough time for each strategy? Were the learning objectives achieved?

Individual participation Did individuals participate in the planning and evaluation process? Were individual learning needs met? Do individuals feel secure and comfortable in the group? Are they allowed to develop at their own pace?

There are six specific planning and evaluation strategies in this book. A number of others can be used as part of the evaluation process. For example, A Woman's Place (see index) can be used at the commencement of a course, and again at the end to ascertain any changes in values and attitudes.

Working with the group

The previous section focussed on the need to plan carefully for all sessions. When working with a group it is essential to acknowledge that the process the group uses is as important as the task it undertakes. The task refers to the goal which the group sets itself, while the process is the manner in which the goal is achieved. In this book we have attempted to address the process as an integral part of achieving any objective.

Group norms During the life of a group, formal and informal rules develop. These rules or group of norms can affect a course in both positive and negative ways. They can relate to the content or issues that the group is allowed to discuss and the activities which are appropriate. Often the norms or rules are unspoken and will only be noticeable when breached. Sometimes the group norms inhibit and constrain participants, at other times positive norms develop which encourage sharing at a very personal level in an atmosphere of trust and support.

When negative or constraining norms develop in a group, the effectiveness of the course will be jeopardized. It will be necessary for you to deal with this situation so that the group can progress. This can be done in a number of ways, such as changing the physical environment, establishing group contracts that specify that during the group new rules apply. Alternatively, bring in a resource person who breaks through the norms; or discuss the situation with the group and ask their advice.

For formal rules to apply, the participants need to participate in their formulation, acknowledge that they exist, and be committed to their implementation.

Roles We all present ourselves to the world in ways that are consistent with our self concept. In groups, participants often take on the same role and repeat the behaviour learned in other groups. As the group continues, members can become trapped into a role which is both detrimental to their own values and to the group. The underlying purpose of the programmes developed in this book is to provide the opportunity for individuals to try out new behaviour and develop different ways of dealing with the world.

Some people always take on a leadership role in a group; they ensure that the task is kept in mind, that issues are clarified or that information is provided. Others may take on the role of carer or nurturer; the person who calms the troubled waters or ensures that everyone else is having a good time. Women traditionally take the nurturing role and it will be important during the course to allow them to try out other behaviours.

Developing a positive working environment A positive working environment is a prerequisite for all of the strategies in this book and is essential if women are to feel supported to make changes in their own lives and the situations around them.

The physical environment is an important influence on the way groups function and each member of the group should feel physically comfortable. Prior to each session, check that the room is set up to assist the group rather than hinder it. If the session is a lecture, panel or film, ensure that everyone can see and hear properly. If an informal discussion is planned, move the tables and arrange the chairs in a circle. Don't attempt a discussion with participants sitting in rows. If you have no choice about the venue, adapt strategies so that they are appropriate to the space available.

The physical setting is only one factor in developing a positive working environment. To establish a climate of trust and acceptance within the group it will be useful to commence with communication, relationship and trust building strategies. With a positive and accepting group it is possible to explore personal issues and increase participation. It is beneficial throughout the course to include trust building activities. Whenever possible, allow members to select their own small working groups for projects and discussions.

In developing a positive working environment it is important to consider the issues of confidentiality, consistency and confrontation. From the very beginning the group and worker can develop a contract which includes expectations about confidentiality, respect for others, observing the right of individuals not to contribute and the validity of all contributions.

Strategies which are selected should be non-competitive and non-threatening and the process should enhance and build rather than diminish self esteem.

Leadership styles It is possible to use the strategies in this book in a range of settings and with a variety of leadership styles. In the past, leaders, youth workers, educators and parents have attempted to direct young people's decision making and development by imposing value systems and lifestyles. The history of the 1960s and 1970s led some people to develop a more laissez-faire approach; let everyone do their own thing. Somewhere between these two is a more appropriate style for workers who want to assist young women to achieve clearer perceptions of reality and greater control over their own lives.

This style includes making it possible for people to examine what might be important to them, helping them make clear in their own minds the options and choices available or desirable, listening with interest to their ideas and thinking, providing information when appropriate, and perhaps challenging when people handicap themselves by limiting their choices.

The role of the worker Working with the group in this way will be a new experience for many workers. It may mean letting go of power, letting other people make mistakes and sometimes taking longer to get the job done. Or it could involve becoming more active and providing greater direction than you have in the past. Flexibility is the key.

A check list for working with the group

- learn the participants' names;
- provide an atmosphere which encourages diversity of opinion;
- develop active listening skills;
- attempt to become non-judgemental and accepting;
- learn to be more comfortable with silences;
- observe the right of individuals not to contribute;
- allow everyone the opportunity to speak;
- encourage participants to respond honestly;
- ask clarifying questions and draw out opinions from the group;
- encourage group members to take responsibility for their own learning;
- assist the group to draw conclusions from their activities and discussions;
- support participants as they try out new behaviour;
- encourage group members to evaluate their own participation and that of the group.

Personal skills: Issues for young women

There are a number of issues and personal skills that young women will become aware of and develop as a result of participating in the kinds of activities suggested in this book.

Self concept and self esteem

The core of an individual's identity is their self concept. The conscious perception she has of herself. Self esteem is the way a person feels about themself, self concept is a contributing factor to self esteem.

The images we hold of ourselves are shaped by such factors as age, race, gender, name, fitness and health. External influences such as culture, religion, social class and personal achievement also contribute. Self concept develops as a result of these factors as well as through identification with others, role expectations, the reactions of others and how they categorise us, especially those close to us.

These images and external factors, and the attitude we develop about our self-worth, combine to make up the positive or negative feelings we experience about self, or self esteem. Studies have shown that women consistently have lower self esteem than men, and this has an effect on their behaviour. High self esteem encourages self respect, satisfying relationships, effective communication skills, independence, the ability to meet personal, social, emotional and economic needs and confidence in personal rights.

In assisting young women to develop positive self esteem it is critical to help them see the effects of outside influences and expectations. It is possible to change negative self image and for women to reach a more realistic image of themselves. It may be a case of unlearning old behaviours and attitudes and replacing them with new ones that are self enriching. Women need affirmation of their self worth and confirmation of their decisions and actions. When working with women's groups:

- Remember that no woman can raise her self esteem by herself. No amount of saying 'You've got to think more highly of yourself' will work.

- Convey recognition of her existence. Women feel invisible when they are confronted by silence when a response is appropriate. It is important not to interrupt, or engage in unrelated activities while she is talking, or listen without conveying any verbal or non-verbal interest.

- Remember that each person is unique. Each woman is individual; she is not a role, an object, a label or stereotype. There is no one else in the world just like her.

- There is no substitute for the direct and honest message: 'You count; you are important; you are important because . . .'.

- Each young woman experiences life in her own way, and her way is not necessarily like yours. It may help to build her esteem by listening to her thoughts and feelings, silences and words. It is not necessary to agree, but accept that this is the way it is for this woman.

- Probably the greatest boost to self esteem is the message: 'I care about you and am willing to be involved in your life'.

It is difficult if you have never experienced low self esteem to understand the feelings and actions of those who do have low self esteem. There is no substitute for empathy and understanding.

Communication skills

Communication is the process by which we give and receive messages. Without communication people could not interact and groups would not function. People are moulded by their communication experiences. In the early years of life communication with important people determines self concept and we learn ways of behaving.

By examining how we communicate we can learn to recognise why we respond to some messages and not others; why we are open to some people and closed to others; why we say the things we do; how our non-verbal and verbal messages affect other people; why we feel comfortable in certain situations and are shy in others and the ways in which we learn best. Through communication we also let others know about ourselves, our values and attitudes.

Verbal communication Verbal messages consist of words, spoken or written, which are structured or patterned. In a group, verbal messages help us to interact socially or pass on information about each other; develop programmes and set goals; make decisions and plan; motivate ourselves to achieve our goals and also to check out with each other and evaluate our performance.

Misunderstandings can occur in verbal communication because we have different understandings of the meanings of words. Unfortunately words do not always convey the meanings we desire. We each give slightly different meanings to words. Another cause of misunderstanding is that sometimes we react negatively or defensively to the way something is expressed, because we don't understand clearly, or because we feel put down or excluded. Racism and sexism are also transmitted through language.

Non-verbal communication It is estimated that verbal messages represent 35% of communication; the largest part, about 65%, is non-verbal. We give the majority of our messages not by what we say but by what we do. We learn a lot about the desires, feelings, beliefs, attitudes and responses of others from their non-verbal messages, and in the same way they learn a lot about us.

Non-verbal messages can emphasise verbal messages; for example, we nod when we say yes, or point when we give directions. They can also provide a substitute for verbal messages; for example, crying, nodding, shrugging or raising an eyebrow. The status of a person in a group can be distinguished by how or where that person sits. Relationships can be indicated; for example, a couple holding hands or sitting with their backs to each other will give different messages. The patterns of interaction in a group can be regulated by nods, hand movements, sitting forward or reclining. Verbal messages can be complemented for example, facial expressions indicate feelings. They can also be contradicted, words can say one thing, while tone and pitch, facial expressions or the way we sit or stand can say something very different.

Some factors which are included in non-verbal communication are facial expressions, eye contact and movement, body movements, posture, hand movements and gestures, feet movements, blushing and sweating. Other factors include place in the environment, where we sit or stand in relation to others, the tone, pitch, and rhythm of the way we say something as well as grunts, sighs, pauses and timing.

Each person has an area around them which constitutes personal space, and when this is invaded people feel uncomfortable. The amount of personal space individuals need differs according to culture, and also whether they live in a city or the country. We can use distance as a way of communicating our feelings. In a group, where we sit can determine how much we talk, and who will dominate. The seating arrangements affect feelings and behaviour.

How we sit and whether we look at people can indicate how we are feeling. When members of the group feel compatible with each other, there is more eye contact and they are more relaxed.

Becoming assertive

As is clear from other material in this book, women are disadvantaged in a wide range of areas including the family, employment, education and the law. One way of dealing with oppression is to lay the blame on the oppressed — blame the victim: If women were more talented, patient, ambitious, etc., then they would achieve success. In the last few years, assertiveness training has become a panacea to overcome women's disadvantage: If women behave assertively they will be treated as equals. This is an over-simplification and ignores the reality of the structural oppression, discrimination and powerlessness that women suffer. However, there are some skills offered in assertivenss training that can assist young women to deal with their situation.

As new attitudes develop towards the role of women in our society, young women find themselves in a dilemma about whether to accept the traditional roles or to move into new ways of relating and behaving. In order for women to change their role, those around them also need to change. It is as though we are all pieces of a jigsaw puzzle, each with our own unique shape.

We are surrounded and contained by others in our lives. If we want to change our shape and take more space, then those around us need to move. This can cause feelings of anxiety, helplessness and powerlessness and many women avoid making changes for fear of the reactions of others.

In a given situation, there are four basic ways to behave — by being indirectly aggressive, directly aggressive, passive or assertive.

Passive behaviour This can be expressed by allowing others to take the initiative in making decisions, rarely expressing opinions, refusing to take initiatives or feeling resentful and self pitying. Women sometimes use these kinds of behaviour as a survival mechanism. We have been socialized to see it as appropriate feminine behaviour. Part of our conditioning is to calm troubled waters and be the peace maker, even if this means denying our own needs.

Indirect aggressive behaviour This occurs when indirect means are used to express feelings, especially anger, or when manipulation is used to achieve an end. This is also discussed as **passive aggressive** behaviour. Women often find themselves in situations where they have no choice but to use this kind of behaviour.

Direct aggressive behaviour This occurs when aggression is expressed openly, either physically or verbally and may include hitting, shouting and overt anger.

Assertive behaviour In this case, views are stated directly, honestly and clearly. It does not exclude anger, but anger is expressed and conveyed in a straightforward manner. It involves making feelings and desires clear in a way that cares for self and others.

Using assertive behaviour involves the expression of positive and negative feelings, limit setting (knowing what space, time and privacy you need and not allowing others to encroach on these), and initiation (knowing what your needs are, and how to express these).

By acting in an assertive way, women can increase their self esteem, diminish their need for approval of others and increase control over their own lives.

Some obstacles to assertiveness are

- lack of awareness about assertive behaviour, we may not realise it is an option;
- anxiety, fear of expressing ourselves even when we know what we want to say;
- low self esteem, we may not think that what we want is worth asking for;
- not having the words to express our feelings and needs;
- having learned behaviour which hinders assertive expression;
- being in situations which make it difficult, sometimes impossible, to act assertively.

Behaving assertively involves learning new behaviour. These include

- verbal messages: express yourself clearly, directly and honestly using 'I' language. That is, make statements that say 'I' rather than 'you' or 'we'. One non-assertive habit is to apologise unnecessarily or to use words which diminish or lessen our value such as 'just a housewife', or 'only a woman';
- non-verbal messages: these should match our verbal messages. The messages we give with our non-verbal communication can totally deny the assertiveness of our words;
- eye contact: women often speak with their eyes averted or head bowed. Hold your head erect and make good eye contact;

- facial expressions: can give strength to a verbal message. Does your face express when you are angry, or do you smile and soften the blow?
- posture: stand and sit straight, be relaxed;
- voice: tone, pitch, inflection and volume should express an assertive attitude;
- body image: feeling good about our body is one step in projecting ourselves assertively;
- compliments and criticism: women have learnt that it is impolite or vain to acknowledge a compliment and often become embarrassed and protest when someone says something nice. We need to practise giving and receiving appropriate compliments. As we become more assertive, it is easier to deal with critical comments. Often criticism is valid and we need to learn how to hear this and deal with it assertively;
- saying no: we need to accept other people's right to say 'no' and learn how to say 'no' ourselves;
- expressing anger: women face a taboo against expressing anger and so do it in a range of un-satisfactory and unproductive ways.

An indirect expression of anger is when we deny our anger, yet take it out on others, perhaps by withholding our affection. A modified expression of anger is when we express annoyance but deny the anger. Depression can be anger unrecognised and turned inward. We have every right to feel anger and to express this assertively. First, we need to recognise our anger, to identify the reason why we are angry, and then to decide how to express the anger.

Checking the influences When we decide to become assertive, we need to examine the influences in our lives and how we deal with them. Some questions to pose:

- who are the people in your life who influence you?
- is the influence positive support or negative constraint?
- how do you respond to a situation — passively, assertively or aggressively?
- do you accept or deny compliments and criticism?
- what patterns are there in the way you react to the people around you?

Giving yourself messages Perhaps the greatest hurdle to overcome in becoming assertive and feeling good about yourself is what is called negative self talk. We constantly give ourselves messages about what we are thinking, feeling and doing. These messages can be positive and esteem building, or negative and diminishing. The first step in building positive esteem and becoming assertive is to catch yourself when you are giving yourself negative messages and change them to positive ones.

Dealing with conflict

One of the many qualities that women develop is that of peacemaker; pouring oil on troubled waters. We are socialized to avoid conflict and disagreeable situations and to make things turn out right. This attitude implies that conflict is bad when in fact conflict is a normal part of living and growing. Without conflict, there would be no change and change itself often creates conflict. If we are going to change and grow, then this will create conflict both within ourselves and with the people around us. When we have options that are equally attractive and we can only choose one, then we experience conflict. The more equally attractive the choices, the greater the conflict.

Often we find ourselves in conflict within ourselves because we have to make a choice or decision about things which are mutually exclusive. Some of these decisions are about simple and relatively unimportant things such as what to wear, while others are more stressful and have long-term effects. These may include what subjects to take in school, what job to accept, whether to phone someone you like, how to say 'no'.

Conflict between people is very often the result of an imbalance in the power within a relationship. When two or more people perceive themselves to be in disagreement about mutually exclusive alternatives, and this disagreement is expressed, then interpersonal conflict exists. Interpersonal conflict or open disagreement need not involve hostility or negative feelings and can be expressed verbally or non-verbally. If the disagreement is brought out into the open, then there is a much better chance of dealing with it and of using it productively.

The attitude we have to being in a group or relationship will influence how we deal with conflict. Some people like to pretend that conflict doesn't exist and avoid it at all costs. This can be damaging both to themselves and others. Other people are competitive and see conflict as something they will either win or lose. If a person sees conflict in this way, then they may not be willing to change their position and may feel put down if they do not win. Issues of self esteem and the role we play will affect how we see ourselves in this win-lose situation.

Another approach to conflict is co-operation. Conflict can help a group achieve its task by raising issues and presenting a range of options; it can be creative, allowing all members an opportunity to test out new ideas. If all the members of a group or the people in a relationship feel that they have gained from the conflict, then it has been productive. The more cohesion and trust in a group, the more likely that conflict, when it occurs, will be dealt with productively.

The **Conflict Continuum** (below) illustrates the ways in which people deal with conflict.

Non-Productive / Productive

Avoidance   Confrontation

Decision making

Decision making is often approached at an emotional level; that is, we operate on a hunch. This is sometimes a good procedure where, without thinking a great deal about it, we can jump from the issue or problem directly to a decision which feels right. Intuition and lateral thinking are valued in creative advertising executives but have been scorned in women. While acknowledging the value of intuition, it is also important to recognise that our lives may be full of uncertainty and confusion if we constantly use this approach to decision making.

Decision making can also be rational and linear; that is, we can explore the choices, examine the consequences and decide on this basis. Most of the strategies in this book use a linear approach to decision making. The most significant reason for this is that it underscores a basic message we have to convey: there are choices. Young women have choices. Learning how to choose and decide raises awareness about areas in which choice is restricted or denied by whatever social constraints may be operating.

Whether or not we make a conscious choice, what we decide is based on what we believe, on what we hold as important values. If the choice is a conscious one, we are more likely to act according to those values we want endorsed by our actions. If the choice is an unconsious one, we will still act according to our values, but quite possibly they will be values unknown to us. It is true that making choices or decisions which are personally satisfying (that is, most true to ourselves) is a skill which can be learned. In addition, like other skills, it must be practised so that we can get better at it, and, like other ways of reasoning, it must be understood so that we can apply it in different situations.

The following is an approach to decision making which can be developed and used with young women.

Decision plan A good basic introduction to decision making can be found in the decision plan. In a decision plan, it is important to break issues down to their component and most basic elements. This may involve thinking about the issue until it can be visualised as two possibilities. Each of these is then considered until two follow-on possibilities can be envisaged and so forth. Eventually, the plan will indicate a variety of options and consequences, and from this information, a decision may be made.

For example, consider a decision plan based on the question: Will I stay in school or go to work next year? The decision to be made is about what I will do next year.

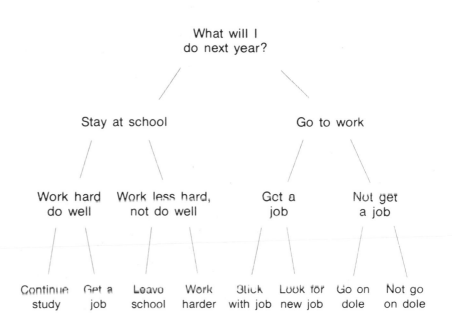

At each level, it is important to ask oneself: what are the alternatives here? If I do this, what will I not do? What are the decisions possible? As you move down the plan, decisions get more and more complex, but the question should be thought of as either *this* or *that*. While it is most helpful to concentrate on action (what can I do, either this or that), one can also look at feelings (how might I react, either this way or that way), or circumstances (how much money will I need, either this much or that much), or outside pressures (what will people say or think).

Priority setting

Priority setting can be described as putting our life goals into order. It utilises both the skills of values clarification and decision making.

The first thing we have to do, if we want to set and live up to our own personal priorities, is to discover what our own values really are. It is often a surprise to discover that we hold particular values. We have to look carefully at those parts of our lives which indicate our true values: how we use our time, how we use our money, where we place our creative and emotional energy, our dreams and goals for our lives, and our patterns of choices and decisions in the past. One useful approach is called values clarification (p.26).

The second thing we have to do, is to examine aspects of significant decisions carefully. 'What will I wear today?' is not a significant decision, but 'Will I dress according to society's code, or will I dress at all?' are decisions of much greater importance. There are a number of key aspects to the skill of decision making, but two of the most important are: recognising when a decision is important, and stopping to think before we act.

The third thing we have to do is learn how to organise our goals in order of importance. We cannot achieve everything we might wish; we must always make choices. We have to learn how to concentrate on the few goals which are most important to us, putting aside for the moment, or perhaps forever, those goals which are less important, so that we can organise our time most usefully and avoid feeling overwhelmed.

There are five steps in setting priorities:

- discovering what we want out of life or a specific situation by exploring images of what we want our life to be;

- having clarified our life goals, we have to organise them in order of importance. This means hard choices and decisions: some goals must be eliminated completely, some set aside for the moment, or for quite a while. Each goal should be refined into realistic steps;

- when priorities are stated and refined as clearly as possible, we need to think about them in terms of difficulty and scope. The end purpose is to choose goals that are satisfying and challenging;

- planning priority action involves drawing up workable plans that will help us achieve these important goals;

- new priorities are set and action steps have been selected. All that is left is to organise our plans into activities we can commence immediately and activities which will be appropriate at a later time.

Techniques

Techniques are specific ways of working with the group. Many of the strategies in this book require an understanding of the techniques described below.

Group discussion

Informal group discussion Group discussion is a technique used often in this book. The skills you will need include the ability to question, explain, clarify, draw out and sum up. If the worker uses these skills effectively, then the group members will be able to discuss issues and reach conclusions themselves.

The size of the group can effect participation. Divide large groups into smaller groups of three to four for more effective discussion. The worker should move from group to group, providing assistance whenever necessary. Allow time for small groups to share their discussions with the large group, and draw together the different strands of discussion when summing up.

Set up the room so that everyone is comfortable and can see and hear each other. The atmosphere should be relaxed; to walk into a room that is empty except for a circle of chairs, can be a little daunting. It can be effective to ask the group to set the room up themselves.

Be aware of different levels of participation in the group. There may be some individuals who dominate; provide opportunities for quiet members to speak, but do not force quiet participants to join the discussion unwillingly. Remember that silence is important. It will be useful if you explain to the group that silences can provide valuable time for reflection. It is important that the worker be comfortable with silences; your example will provide an important model for others.

Encourage participants to use their own personal experience rather than generalising, speaking about other people, or talking theoretically. Be sure that people do not interrupt each other. Being listened to without interruption is esteem building.

It can be helpful when everyone in the group is expressing the same opinions, to stimulate discussion by taking the role of Devil's Advocate. For example, 'It could be argued that . . . or 'I could put a case for . . .' is better than assuming a position which is not your own.

The discussion will work if you have set yourself clear objectives. It is possible to lead a group through a complete topic in logical sequence by presenting new points to the group when necessary.

Structured group discussion In addition to informal discussion techniques, more structured kinds of discussion can also be useful. When the subject is controversial, or to encourage expression of a wide range of views, structured discussion techniques can stimulate the group to broaden their thinking. Traditional debating techniques can be utilised, or the concept can be modified to allow less competitive debate.

Brainstorming

Brainstorming is a dynamic way of generating the maximum number of ideas in the shortest possible time, with total group participation. It is fun, and can be used to generate common definitions, plan programs or as a warm up activity in a quiet group.

For brainstorming to be successful, it is vital to adhere to three simple rules:

- accept every idea and write it down;
- aim for quantity not quality;
- no discussion.

The procedure is:

- decide on a topic;
- state the topic clearly to the group;
- appoint a recorder, or recorders to list all the ideas as they are called out;
- state the rules clearly and enforce them as the brainstorm proceeds;
- restate the topic and the time limit;
- indicate when the time is up.

Set and enforce a time limit of no more than ten minutes. At the end of this, go through the lists with the group and code the responses as appropriate. Allow time for general discussion. Brainstorming may be done in a large group of 15-20, or in smaller groups which come together at the end to share and discuss their results.

Values clarification

Women are constantly bombarded with messages about what to do, think and feel. These are often confusing or conflicting. It is not always easy to work out what we believe in and value. In order to aid this process, a technique called values clarification has been developed. It is used frequently in this book.

Values clarification is an approach developed initially by Louis Raths, and later expanded and further developed by others, chiefly Sidney Simon. The core of this approach is the valuing process. Values clarification is not about content of values, but about the process. The assumption is that if one can learn the skill of valuing, that skill can be applied to choices and decisions throughout life. The valuing process has seven sub-processes or categories. The seven valuing sub-processes are:

Choosing

(1) choosing freely. If circumstance, authority or the situation limits choice, there is no real choice and we cannot value what we choose. An imposed choice is not a free choice.

(2) choosing from alternatives: one of the most important parts of valuing is the generation of alternatives, seeing what possibilities exist.

(3) choosing after careful consideration of the consequences of each alternative: having discovered what alternatives exist, it is possible to consider what would happen if we were to choose each alternative. The choice we make after considering consequences may not be the most desirable choice, but it may be the most responsible or the most satisfying. The more thought given to our choices and the options and consequences, the more we will have pride in our eventual decisions.

Prizing

(4) prizing and cherishing, learning to take reasonable pride in our choices and to feel good about our decisions.

(5) affirming: feeling good about our choices means that we can affirm them to ourselves, or to others. The more public the affirmation, the more important the choice will appear.

Acting

(6) acting upon the value: perhaps the most contentious part of the Raths approach is the assumption that only those values acted upon are true values. The choices we make reflect values in action.

(7) acting with a pattern: to be able to look at our lives, our actions, our choices and decisions, and detect a repeated pattern which indicates what we truly value.

A number of guidelines are important when using values clarification:

- everyone has the right not to contribute;
- people deserve the right to decide whether or not they wish to participate in discussion of their values. This is sometimes called 'offering a contract';
- the leader participates, but, like everyone else, she has the right to pass if she wishes;
- an answer a person gives may be explored and clarified, but should neither be denied nor questioned. It represents the right answer for that person at that time, the one she has chosen.

Working with a group exploring values can be a difficult experience; it requires patience and support from the worker. Be certain that the subject is appropriate for values clarification. If you want to take a convincing or persuasive position, then don't use this technique. For example, never use it when trying to convince a group that rape is always wrong. Values clarification can provide a rewarding experience for group participants and the worker; it helps people to sort out the complexities of life and to choose the things they value.

Role play

Role play is an educational technique which enables individuals to explore emotions, reactions, thoughts, behaviours, attitudes and values. Participation in role play can provide opportunities to experience a given situation, reflect on the situation and gain greater understanding of the experience. It is about trying on new roles and testing them, something children know how to do from their very early years. Playing mothers and fathers, dress up or school, are ways children test out how it feels to be in these new or different situations.

As an educational technique, it depends on the ability of the participants to overcome shyness and rely on their creativity. It is not always appropriate and cannot overcome all problems. It also depends on the skills of the worker. It has the potential to increase communication skills and to build self esteem; the shared experience of role play can bring the group closer together.

When using role play, involve all participants in some way, and be sure to have well defined objectives. What do you want to achieve as a result of the role play?

Preparation is vital: one-fifth of the total time should be spent in preparing the group. Use warm up and movement activities to relax participants and create the mood. Never force an unwilling person to participate; rather call on volunteers to take certain roles. Use some way of identifying participants in their roles; hats, tags, or costumes can do this.

The role play will not happen by itself; the worker will need to take the job of stage manager. Ask participants to take their role seriously, and keep encouraging the players to stay in their role to explore the situation fully.

Observers to the role play might be prepared by developing observation questions such as: what sort of people were they (in the play)?, what feelings did they convey?, what happened?, why?, how did players react to each other?

Perhaps the most important part of role play is de-roling. At the end of the role play, each player discusses how they felt in the role, and what happened to them. Then each player sheds the role. This can be symbolised by taking off the costume, hat, tag or other identifying props. De-roling is then complete and players must not be referred to as the character, or by the character's name, but by their own name.

Debriefing is the period during which reflection and evaluation occur. Be sure to allow for this period. As themselves, players discuss what they learned from the experience. Observers contribute their observations and general discussion takes place about the relevance of these experiences to their own lives.

Background Reading

Whitelegg, Elizabeth et al., *The changing Experience of Women,* Martin Robertson/O.U., 1982.

Adler, Sue and Cornbleet, Annie, *Anti-sexist resources guide,* ILEA Publishing Centre, 1984. Lists womens organisations, bookshops, publishers, films, videos and other resources as well as facilities within the ILEA.

Archer, John and Lloyd, Barbara, *Sex & Gender,* Penguin, 1981.

Waiting Our Turn: Working with women in youth clubs, N. Ireland Association of Youth Clubs.

Yeung, K., *Working with Girls _ a readers route map,* National Youth Bureau, 1985.

Hemmings, Susan, *A wealth of experience: The lives of older women,* Pandora, 1985.

GEN, *Anti-sexist education magazine,* Women's Education Group.

McRobbie, Angela and McCabe, Trisha (eds.), *Feminism for Girls: An adventure story,* Routledge & Kegan Paul, 1981.

Bristol Women's Studies Group, *Half the Sky An introduction for women's studies,* Virago, 1979.

Coote, Anna and Campbell, Beatrix, *Sweet Freedom: The struggle for women's liberation,* Picador, 1982.

Simon, Sydney et al, *Values Clarification*, Hart Publishing Co. Inc., 1972.

Resources

Some Girls, NAYC Publications Dept. Set of Booklets intended to promote discussion about issues such as periods, harassment, female solidarity.

Ninvalle, Natalle, *Changing Images,* Sheba Feminist Publishers, 1984. A collection of anti-sexist and anti-racist drawings which can be photocopied.

Novels

We can learn a lot from reading about the lives and experiences of women in novels. Stories and novels by women are too numerous to mention and It is worth writing to the specific women's publishers for their current catalogue. Addresses can be found in the address section at the end of the book.

Look particularly for books from:

> Virago
> Womens Press
> Sheba Feminist Publishers

as well as the mainstream publishers.

Getting It All Together

This section provides practical strategies for working with the group as detailed in the previous section. The first six strategies are about planning and evaluation. The next ten provide ways for individuals in the group to get to know and feel comfortable with each other. The last five strategies will assist in developing communication skills.

Strategies

Sharing expectations
Evaluation voting
Unfinished sentences
Evaluation game
Evaluation symbols
Magic box
And my mother's name is . . .
Name tags
Moving groups
Photographs
Creative introduction

This is my best friend
I'd like you to meet
Things I like about you
What I like best about me
Swap shop
Strengths
This is me
Non-verbal lucky dip
Active listening
Brag session
Assertive body language
Put downs

Sharing expectations

Objectives:
- To introduce the idea of self-directed learning.
- To gain information from the group for course planning.
- To make the content of the course relevant to as many group members as possible.

Prerequisites: Literacy skills.

Time needed: 30-45 minutes.

What you need: A copy of 'Sharing expectations worksheet' (p.33) for each participant, felt tip pens, flipchart paper.

What you do:
(a) Hand each participant a copy of the worksheet and ask them to complete it. Ask each person to keep their worksheet so that this can be referred to during the course.

(b) When each person has finished, form small groups of 4-6. Ask each group to appoint a recorder. The task is now to make a composite list of expectations and to select priorities. Emphasise that individuals do not have to read out their own lists unless they choose to do so. The recorder makes a list.

(c) When the list is complete, ask the group to mark those most mentioned. It is useful to develop a code for topics most mentioned, high priorities, ones of lower priority, realistic, unrealistic, etc.

(d) Bring the small groups back together and ask a volunteer from each group to read out their list. Develop a list for the whole group and highlight the priorities.

Sharing expectations worksheet

For me this group will be:

I really want to learn:

By the end of this course I will have:

I joined this group because:

In this group I want to:

We should talk about:

I might not want to talk about:

Evaluation voting

Objectives:
- To make a public statement about the session or course.
- To move and have fun.
- To collect information from the group which will assist with future planning.

Prerequisites: Participation in the session or course.

Time needed: 5 minutes.

What you need: Nothing.

How you do it: (a) Explain that you will read out a statement (see suggestions below) and that people should respond quickly with hand signals, not allowing time to think too much or debate. It is an instant reaction and represents how a person thinks right now. Later their answer may well be different. Explain the hand signals.

(b) Read the statements. In this activity it is useful for the worker to participate, but delay your voting slightly because it is possible for you to influence group members.

Suggested questions: How many of you
- enjoyed the session;
- feel comfortable and relaxed;
- would like to know more about the subject;
- would like to move on to a different subject;
- enjoyed the film;
- understood the topic;
- have changed your opinion about this issue.

Note: Develop specific questions to relate to the actual session.

Unfinished sentences

Objectives:
- To gain immediate reaction from participants about a session
- To check that the session is meeting the participants' expectations.

Prerequisites: Participation in the session. Literacy skills.

Time needed: 10-15 minutes.

What you need: A copy of the unfinished sentences and a pen for each participant.

What you do:
(a) Select four appropriate unfinished sentences and space them on a sheet.

(b) Hand out the unfinshed sentences to each participant.

(c) Ask each participant to complete the sentences. Explain that these sheets will be handed in and they do not have to sign them. Stress that it is important that they be honest in their response

(d) Collect the sheets and collate the responses. If the group is continuing, they may like to see the collated responses.

Examples of unfinished sentences:
Right now I feel . . .
Next session I hope . . .
The best thing about this session was . . .
One thing I really liked was . . .
I wish I could . . .
I think we could have . . .
I learned . . .
One thing I didn't like was . . .
I would change . . .
Next time we . . . ,
This session has been . . .

Evaluation — field of words

Objectives: ● To find out how the group members are feeling about the session or the course.

Prerequisites: Participation in the session.

Time needed: 10 minutes.

What you need: A field of words worksheet for each participant.

What you do: (a) Explain that you will hand out a sheet with words written on it that describe feelings and reactions. Participants may be more honest if anonymity is made optional.

(b) Ask the participants to circle the words that best describe their feelings about the session. They can add their own words if they can't find suitable words on the sheet.

(c) Collect the sheets when they are completed. If the group is continuing, they may like to see the collated response.

Field of words — worksheet

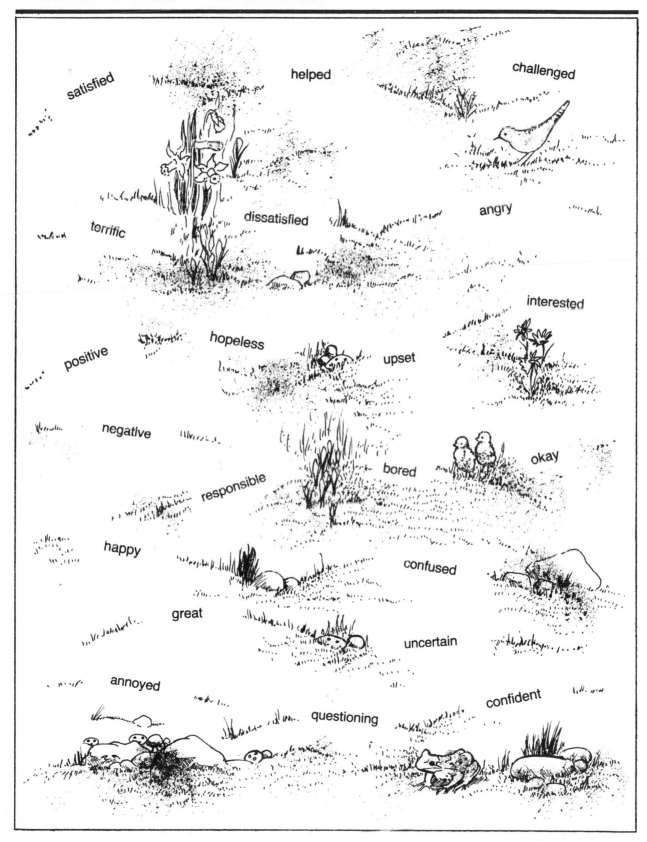

satisfied

helped

challenged

angry

terrific

dissatisfied

interested

positive

hopeless

upset

negative

okay

responsible

bored

happy

confused

great

uncertain

annoyed

questioning

confident

Evaluation symbols

Objectives:
- To elicit feedback from the group on their reactions to the course.
- To draw the group together and provide a positive focus to conclude the course.

Prerequisites: Participation in the course.

What you need: Nothing.

Time needed: 20-30 minutes.

How you do it:
(a) At a previous session ask participants to think about what the course has meant to them and bring something to symbolise this to the group.

(b) At the conclusion of the last session, form a circle and ask participants to place their symbol in the centre of the circle.

(c) Provide time for each person to express their feelings about the course and the meaning of their symbol, if they so choose.

Magic box

Objectives:
- To dream.
- To share ideals and hopes.
- To evaluate and plan for the future.

Prerequisites: This strategy can be useful to evaluate a course. If using it this way, make the wish specific to the session.

Time needed: 10-20 minutes.

What you need: Nothing.

What you do:

(a) Ask the group to form a circle.

(b) Tell them that there is a magic invisible box in the centre of the circle; that the box has the power to grant any wish that it chooses, and that today it will grant each person in the room one wish.

(c) Ask for a volunteer to start by making their wish out loud. The wishes may be for knowledge, skills, change or anything they can think of.
Continue around the circle until everyone has had an opportunity to make their wish.

And my mother's name is . . .

Objectives:
- To reduce nervousness in a new group.
- To get to know each other.
- To learn each other's names.
- To introduce our mothers.
- To have fun.

Prerequisites: None.

Time needed: 10-15 minutes.

What you need: Nothing.

What you do:

(a) Ask the group to sit in a circle.

(b) Explain that we usually introduce ourselves with our own name and that of our father or husband. Our family name, surname or last name comes from the male side of our families. This activity allows us to introduce our mothers and affirm the female side of our families.

(c) The person to start introduces herself and the name of her mother. Example: My name is Elizabeth and mother's name is (was) Joan.

(d) The next person introduces the person before and then herself. Example: This is Elizabeth, I am Mary and my mother's name is (was) Kim.

(e) The third person introduces the previous two and then herself and so on, until the entire circle has been introduced.

Variation: Introduce mother's family name.

Name tags

Objectives: ● To get to know each other.

● To make positive statements about ourselves.

Prerequisites: Literacy skills.

Time needed: 20-30 minutes.

What you need: Paper, at least 15 cm (6") square, pins, felt tip pens.

What you do:
(a) Give paper, pins and pen to each person.

(b) Ask each person to write their name in the middle of the paper.

(c) Explain the procedure by telling them to write in each corner of the paper as you read out the instruction. Be sure to leave enough time between instructions for each person to finish writing.

(d) In the top left hand corner ask participants to write their favourite activity; in the bottom left hand corner complete the sentence 'The best thing about me is . . . .'; in the top right hand corner the name of a woman they admire; in the bottom right hand corner their greatest achievement or attribute.

(e) Each person then pins their 'name tag' on to their chest. The leader must be a participant in this activity.

(f) Ask everyone to stand up, and move around the room, reading each other's tags and discussing what is written on them. Be sure that everyone meets each other this way before finishing. If people seem to be staying with the same person, encourage them to move on.

(g) When you think that everyone has had enough time, finish the discussion.
Note: This strategy can be followed by 'I'd like you to meet.' (p.47).

Moving groups

Objectives:	● To get to know each other.
	● To have fun.
Prerequisites:	None.
Time needed:	15-30 minutes.
What you need:	A large clear space.
What you do:	(a) Ask participants to form into groups around an identifying feature, e.g. the colour of the shoes they are wearing (see below for others).
	(b) When the groups have formed, allow three or four minutes for them to talk together and then share the discussion with the large group.
	(c) Repeat with three or four more identifying features.

Some identifying features:
  colour of eyes/hair
  area in which they live
  country or city of birth
  age group
  position in the family
  hair style
  favourite leisure activity
  living arrangements

Photographs

Objectives: ● To show how people perceive each other.

Prerequisites: None.

Time needed: 15-20 minutes.

What you need: Nothing.

What you do:
(a) Ask the group to form into pairs.

(b) Tell them that they will be asked to spend thirty seconds to one minute looking at each other, in order to take an imaginary photograph that they will describe to each other.

(c) At the end of thirty seconds or one minute, ask them to close their eyes and, turn, describe the 'photo' of what they saw.

(d) When both partners have finished, allow time for discussion on how accurate the perceptions were and the assumptions we make about each other from our perceptions.

(e) Reform the group for discussion and summing up.

Creative introduction

Objectives:
- To allow group members to share something of themselves.
- To encourage creative expression.
- To develop a different mode of communication.

Prerequisites: None.

Time needed: 30-45 minutes.

What you need: Sheets of flipchart paper, glue, scissors, sticky tape, magazines, access to the outside environment or plasticine.

What you do:

(a) Explain to the group that they are going to introduce themselves by creating a personal collage or sculpture. It should be abstract, and portray some aspects of themselves that they would like to share.

(b) Allow 15-20 minutes for group members to wander outside collecting pods, leaves, twigs — whatever takes their fancy, but without destroying the environment.

(c) The next step is for them to put together their collage or make their sculpture.

(d) When they have finished, have each person in turn explain their work, and tell what they want to about their portrayal.

As this is a personal expression, encourage other group members to listen, and not to probe too much because there may be some things that a person does not want to share.

Note: Participants may like to keep their creation and bring them to the last session as part of the evaluation.

This is my best friend

Objectives:
- To provide an introductory activity.
- To have participants consider their strengths and see themselves from their friends' point-of-view.

Prerequisite: Best done about the 4th or 5th session.

Time needed: 30 minutes.

What you need: A copy of the 'This is my best friend worksheet' (p.46) for each participant.

What you do:
(a) Give each participant a pen and a copy of the worksheet.

(b) Ask each participant to fill out the sheet as though they are their best friend; they can think of a specific person or imagine what they would like a friend to say.

(c) Ask the group to sit in a large circle and introduce themselves to the group. As it is each person's turn, they stand behind their chair and take the role of the best friend; as though they are still sitting in the chair.

(d) Ask the group to comment on how they feel about the activity.

This is my best friend — worksheet

The reason .... is my best friend is because she is:

She is really good at

I like the way she

Sometimes she gets cross about

She really hopes that one day she will

Other things I like about her are:

Something I don't like about her is:

I'd like you to meet . . .

Objectives:
- To get to know each other.
- To develop listening skills.
- To make a public presentation to the group.
- To hear how we are seen by others.
- To practise speaking clearly and assertively.

Prerequisites: None.

Time needed: 30 minutes.

What you need: Nothing.

What you do:

(a) Ask the group to form into pairs.

(b) Explain the strategy by saying that the first person in each pair spends about 5 minutes talking about herself. The listener may draw out or ask questions, but essentially it is that person's job to listen and learn as much as possible about the speaker.

(c) After the time is up, call for the pairs to switch roles, and repeat the above step.

(d) After another five minutes, ask pairs to join with another pair.

(e) Each person in turn introduces their partner, sharing what they have learned from their discussion, until everyone in the four has been introduced.

Variation: Allow partners to spend more time together and develop a creative way to introduce each other.

Introduce partners to the whole group. This requires more confidence in public speaking and more time.

Things I like about you

Objective: ● To practise giving and receiving compliments.

Prerequisites: None.

Time needed: 20-30 minutes.

What you need: Nothing.

What you do:

(a) Ask each person to find a partner, someone they feel comfortable with.

(b) Explain that we often find it difficult to give compliments but we usually find it even more difficult to receive them. When we are paid a compliment, we usually brush it off, say 'It's nothing' or become embarrassed. For many of us, this exercise will be difficult as we have learnt that it is immodest or vain to feel good about ourselves and even worse to say so.

(c) Taking turns, each person is to pay the other a compliment such as, 'I really like the way you do your hair'. The response should acknowledge the compliment. For example, 'I'm so glad you noticed my hair, thank you'. Or 'Thank you for commenting on my hair, I changed the style last week'.

(d) Allow time for each pair to pay each other and acknowledge 3-4 compliments.

(e) In groups of four, discuss the problems that participants had in receiving compliments; the positive feelings they had and why we are trained not to feel positive about our good points.

What I like best about me

Objectives:
- To help participants clarify their self image.
- To determine what they most value about themselves.
- To practise assertive communication.

Prerequisites: None.

Time Needed: 40-45 minutes.

What you need: 'What I like best about me worksheet' and pen for each participant.

What you do:
(a) Ask participants to get into a comfortable position and close their eyes. As they relax, ask them to think about words or phrases that best describe them.

(b) After about five minutes — or when they seem finished — ask them to open their eyes and write eight of the words and phrases in the spaces provided on the worksheet.

(c) When completed, ask them to rank the words and phrases with the one they like most at the top and the one they like least at the bottom.

(d) Give participants plenty of time to complete the ranking and to consider what they would like to do about the order and the words they like least. Do they want to make any changes? How will they go about this? Were they surprised about the order?

(e) Ask participants to complete the sentence stems on the worksheets.

(f) In small groups of three, ask each participant to share what they like most about themselves and practise saying this in a confident and assertive way.

Note: This activity could be followed by Swap Shop (p.51).

What I like best about me — worksheet

What I like best about me

1 ....

2 ....

3 ....

4 ....

5 ....

6 ....

7 ....

8 ....

What I like least about me

I was surprised that ....

....

....

Things I would most like to change ....

....

....

I will do this by ....

....

....

Swap shop

Objective:
- To provide opportunities for participants to think about changes they might like to make in themselves.

Prerequisites: What I like best about me.

Time needed: 15 minutes.

What you need: Nothing.

What you do:

(a) Explain to the participants that today there is a magic swap shop open in the building. Each participant is going to be able to purchase or obtain qualities that they would like to have or increase. In order to do this, they need to swap qualities that they already have.

(b) Ask participants to consider what qualities they would like or would like more of, and what qualities they are willing to swap in order to get these.

(c) Ask each participant to state clearly what they would like to achieve and what they are willing to exchange for it.

(d) Discuss whether it is possible for people to change their personalities or develop new qualities and how this might be achieved.

Strengths

Objectives:
- For participants to practise introducing themselves in a confident manner.
- To provide an opportunity for participants to say positive things about themselves.

Prerequisites: This activity is best preceeded by another activity which has left the group standing.

Time needed: 30-40 minutes.

What you need: Nothing.

What you do:

(a) Ask participants all together to say their names loudly, sadly, angrily, happily, etc. This will create a babble of noise.

(b) Ask them to think about the way in which they like to hear their name or say their name.

(c) Ask the participants to get into pairs and introduce themselves to their partner. 'My name is . . .' in a range of moods (e.g. angry, sad, happy) and volumes (e.g. loud, soft . . .).

(d) Ask each pair to discuss the experience, considering the ways they feel most comfortable.

(e) Now ask each person in the pair to introduce themselves and add one thing they like about themselves without giggling or whispering. 'My name is . . . and one thing I like about myself is . . .'

(f) Ask the group to form a circle and each person introduce themselves to the group adding the thing they like about themselves.

(g) In the large group, discuss why we find it difficult to say positive things about ourselves.

This is me

Objectives:
- To provide participants with the opportunity to think about their positive points.
- To check these out with another person.

Prerequisites: None.

Time needed: 50 minutes.

What you need: A pen, and copy of the 'This is me worksheet' for each participant.

What you do:

(a) Hand each participant a copy of the worksheet and ask them to code each statement as they see themselves. When finished, have them fold the sheet in half.

(b) Ask participants to find a partner in the group, someone they know well and feel comfortable with.

(c) Have the partners swap sheets and fill in the second column for each other. They should then open the sheets and discuss the differences and similarities explaining and checking any differences in interpretation.

(d) Ask each participant to think about the two lists and complete the sentence at the bottom of the page.

(e) Discuss the positive outcomes of the exercise.

This is me — worksheet

Here are some statements that may or may not describe you. Using the code, rate your-self. Try not to use 2 or 4 too often. When you have finished fold the paper in half and ask someone else in the group to rate how they see you.

Your codes:
I've lots of energy
I enjoy trying new things
I have a good sense of humour
I'm easy to approach
I have strong feelings
I do well at work/school
I enjoy reading
I make friends easily
I am relaxed
I worry a lot
I am good fun
I am confident
I'm a happy person
I have a healthy body
I am pleasant to look at
I'm shy
I'm a good talker
I listen well
I have good taste
I'm a 'together person'
Other ....

Your friend's codes:
Lots of energy
Enjoys trying new things
Good sense of humour
Easy to approach
Has strong feelings
Does well at work/school
Enjoys reading
Makes friends easily
Is relaxed
Worries a lot
Is good fun
Is confident
Is a happy person
Has a healthy body
Is pleasant to look at
Is shy
Is a good talker
Listens well
Has good taste
Is a 'together person'
Other ....

Code
Very much like me   1
Sometimes like me   2
Never like me   3
I don't know   4

I see myself as a ....

.... person.

Non-verbal lucky dip

Objectives:
- To increase participants' awareness of non-verbal communication.
- To provide participants with the opportunity to both express and identify non-verbal cues of attitudes and feelings.

Prerequisites: Some discussion of non-verbal communication.

Time needed: 20-30 minutes.

What you need: Envelopes with instructions in each (see p.56).

What you do:
(a) Ask for eight volunteers.
(b) Each volunteer draws an envelope and then behaves in the way described.
(c) The rest of the group write down what they think is the attitude expressed.
(d) Answers are shared and the cues are written onto a flip chart or board.
(e) Ask participants to name other attitudes or feelings and describe the non-verbal cues that would communicate those.
(f) Provide each participant with the opportunity to practise a variety of non-verbal responses.

Variation: Divide the group into pairs and have them communicate non-verbally a range of feelings and attitudes.

Non-verbal cues

Defensiveness
Arms crossed on chest
Crossing legs
Fistlike gestures
Pointing index finger
Karate chops

Co-operation and Interest
Upper body in sprinter's position
Open hands
Sitting on edge of chair
Hand-to-face gestures
Unbuttoning coat
Tilted head

Frustration
Short breaths
'Tsk' sound
Tightly clenched hands
Wringing hands
Fistlike gestures
Pointing index finger
Rubbing hand through hair
Rubbing back of neck

Criticism
Squinting
Chewing pencil/pen
Leaning forward
Frowning
General tension

Nervousness and Insecurity
Clearing throat
Whistling
Cigarette smoking
Picking or pinching flesh
Fidgeting
Hand over mouth while speaking
Not looking at other person
Perspiring, wringing of hands

Suspicion and Fear
Arms crossed
Sideways glance
Touching, rubbing nose
Rubbing eyes
Buttoning coat, drawing away

Boredom
Lack of communication
Reclining position
Yawning
Sighing
Eyes wandering
Attention diverting

Confidence
Steepled hands
Hands behind back
Back stiffened
Hands in pockets with thumbs out
Hands on lapels of coat

Active listening

Objectives:
- To explore the importance of active listening.
- To provide participants with practice in listening.
- To increase listening skills.

Prerequisites: An introduction to communication; or an activity such as 'Taking a stand' (p.161).

Time needed: 20-30 minutes.

What you need: A list of possible topics.

What you do:

(a) Ask each participant to choose a partner and find themselves a space.

(b) Select a topic from the list and explain to the group that the pairs are to discuss this topic.

(c) Before they start, ask one of the pair to be the speaker and the other to be the listener. The listeners are asked not to listen, not to look at the speaker, but to lean back and fidget. After two minutes change roles. Ask each pair to discuss how they felt as the speaker and what messages they received; how the listener felt and the problems they had listening

(d) Now repeat the exercise but ask the listener to sit in a relaxed open position and lean forward. The listener should make eye contact with the speaker. After both have had a turn, ask them to discuss the difference.

(e) Ask the pairs to consider the ways in which we know someone is listening to us. One way is when someone checks out what we are saying or summarises and then responds. Ask each pair to listen carefully and then summarise the substance of what is being said and then respond before moving on to the next point.

(f) After two minutes, change roles.

(g) After another two minutes, ask the pairs to discuss the whole exercise, noting what they learned about the difficulties of listening and what was good about having someone really listen.

(h) Share the experience in a large group.

Possible topics

- a woman's place in the home;
- married women shouldn't work;
- women have more choices than men;
- men work harder than women;
- women are more emotional than men;
- when I am angry, I . . . ;
- the nicest thing that happened to me last week was . . .

Brag Session

Objectives:
- To explore the reasons why women find it difficult to say positive things about themselves. To provide participants with the opportunity to 'brag'.

Prerequisites: None.

Time needed: 30 minutes.

What you need: Nothing.

What you do:
(a) Divide the group into small groups of 3 or 4 and outline the rules of brainstorming (see p.25).

(b) Ask participants to brainstorm all the words and phrases that they associate with the word 'brag'.

(c) After five minutes, have each group share their lists and discuss why it is usually seen as negative for women to brag; to say positive things about themselves.

(d) Again in the small groups, participants brainstorm all the positive things that people could feel and say about themselves.

(e) Ask each participant to select three of the positive words or statements that apply to themself and share them with other members of the small group.

(f) Discuss the difficulties that participants have in 'bragging' or saying positive things about themselves.

Assertive body language

Objectives:
- To observe the way in which body language affects verbal messages, particularly when the verbal and non-verbal messages don't match.
- To practise assertive non-verbal communication.

Prerequisites: None.

Time needed: 15-30 minutes.

What you need: Nothing.

What you do:

(a) Ask each participant to find a partner and stand in a space away from others.

(b) Ask each pair to practise body language from the following list:
- discuss a controversial topic with hands held together or behind your back;
- discuss the same topic with clenched fists, hands on hips; arms folded across your chest;
- make a request such as — could you lend me your book, with your head bowed and eyes averted; with little sideways glances; with head erect and good eye contact;
- tell your partner that you are very angry with them while you are smiling; then in a whisper;
- tell your partner that you really like them; in a loud voice; with your hands on your hips; in a soft voice; looking at the ceiling.

(c) Ask the pairs to discuss the experience and the difficulties of communicating and continue these discussions in the large group.

(d) Ask participants to identify the non-verbal behaviours that express assertiveness. Include posture, facial expressions, eye contact, gestures, voice tone, pitch and pace and proximity.

(e) In the same pairs, ask participants to practise communicating assertively, by making a simple request, expressing anger, caring, concern and friendship.

(f) In the large group, discuss the differences between passive, aggressive and assertive body language and communication and why women find it difficult to communicate assertively.

Put downs

Objectives:
- To discuss the range of ways in which women are 'put down'.
- To develop responses to these.
- To practise assertive communication.

Prerequisites: None.

Time needed: 40-50 minutes.

What you need: Large sheets of flip chart paper and felt tip pens.

What you do:
(a) Divide the large group into small groups of 4 or 5 and explain the rules of brainstorming (see p.25).

(b) Ask the groups to brainstorm all the ways in which they are 'put down', both physically and verbally.

(c) Share the lists in the large group, make a composite list and discuss the settings in which these 'put downs' are used.

(d) Ask each of the small groups to select 3 or 4 of the put downs, discuss ways of responding to them. Prepare a role play to demonstrate their responses.

(e) Each group presents their role play to the large group. Discuss the responses and practise ways of being more assertive. Ensure that each participant has the opportunity to practise responding assertively.

Variation: Brainstorm and discuss the ways in which women put themselves down and practise ways of changing these.

Background Reading

Satow, Antoinette and Evans, Martin, *Working with Groups*, HEC/TACADE 1982

Douglas, Tom, *Basic Group Work*, Tavistock, 1978.

Hopson, Barry and Scally, Mike, *Lifeskills Teaching*, McGraw-Hill, 1981.

Jacques, David, *Learning in Groups*, Croom Helm, 1984.

Taylor, Bryce, *Experiential Learning: A framework for Group Skills*, Oasis Publications, 1983.

Dickson, Ann, *A woman in your own right*, Quartet, 1982.

Ernst, Sheila and Goodison, Lucy, *In our own hands: A book of self-help therapy*, Womens Press, 1981.

Canfield, J. and Wells, H. *100 ways to enhance self-concept in the classroom*, Prentice Hall, 1976.

Resources

Brandes, Donna and Phillips, Howard, *Gamesters Handbook*, Hutchinson, 1979.

Brandes, Donna, *Gamesters 2*, Hutchinson, 1982.

Girl Talk, colour video (15 mins), Connexions, 1984.

Growing Up Female

Socialization is the process through which individuals learn the values, expectations and rules of the society to which they belong. Most social scientists acknowledge that socialization is a complex process involving a range of institutions such as the family, language, school, religion and the media.

'Growing up female' includes strategies which focus on language, the family and religion and the way in which they influence our perceptions and expectations as we grow up female.

Strategies

A womans place

Girls and boys go out to play

The typical Briton

The family tree

Herstory

The man in the moon

Women gossip, men talk

Opposite and unequal

Why can't a woman

Getting it right

The sins of the mothers

If I was

Messages

Women in songs

A woman's place

Objectives:
- To make a public statement about female and male roles in society.
- To introduce movement into the programme.
- To demonstrate the range of opinions in the group.

Prerequisites: None. A good introductory activity.

Time needed: 10 minutes.

What you need: Nothing.

What you do: (a) Explain the hand signals.

(b) Explain that you will read out a statement (see suggestions below), and that people should respond quickly with hand signals, not allowing time to think too much or debate. It is an instant reaction and represents how a person thinks right now. At another time, answers may be different.

(c) Read the statements. In this activity, the worker should also participate, but delay your voting slightly so as not to influence group members.

Note: Other statements can be designed about a range of topics.

Suggested statements:
- Boys should have more education than girls.
- Women and men should equally share child raising.
- Women should not work on night shifts.
- Husbands should earn more than their wives.
- Women should be responsible for the housework.
- Women are more emotional than men.
- Women don't make good bosses.
- Men should never cry.
- Nursing is a woman's job.
- Men are not capable of caring for small children.
- Women can't do heavy manual work.

Girls and boys go out to play

Objectives:	• To explore the different attitudes to female and male behaviour during childhood.
	• To initiate a discussion on sex role socializaion.
Prerequisites:	Literacy skills.
Time needed:	30 minutes.
What you need:	A copy of 'Girls and boys go out to play Sentence Stems' and pen for each participant.
What you do:	(a) Hand out the sentence stems (p.66).
	(b) Explain that this is not a test and that there are no right or wrong answers.
	(c) Ask participants to complete the sentence stems with the first thoughts that come to them.
	(d) When participants have finished, ask them to look at their answers. Do they see differences in what they have written for girls and boys?
	(e) In small groups, ask participants to discuss their different attitudes to female and male behaviour. How do these attitudes develop?
	(f) Share these discussions in the large group.
Further activity:	Collect some examples of reading schemes and young childrens books and get the group to look at the implied male and female behaviour in them.

Boys and girls go out to play — sentence stems

Little girls always ....

Little boys always ....

Big girls never ....

Big boys never ....

Girls like ....

Boys like ....

The games girls like best ....

....

The games boys like best ....

....

The reason girls like to play ....

is because ....

The reason boys like to play ....

is because ....

When a girl starts to grow up, she becomes ....

....

When a boy starts to grow up, he becomes ....

....

The typical Briton

Objective: ● To explore stereotypes of women and men in British society.

Prerequisites: None.

Time needed: 45-50 minutes.

What you need: Large sheets of flipchart paper and coloured felt tip pens or magazines, scissors and glue.

What you do:
(a) Divide the large group into small groups of three or four participants.

(b) Provide each small group with paper and felt tip pens or magazines, scissors and glue.

(c) Ask the groups to draw or make a collage of the 'typical Briton'.

(d) When each group has finished, display the pictures and have a representativo from each group explain what characteristics they identified for a 'typically British person'.

(e) Ask the participants to identify common themes. How realistic are these given the multi-racial nature of our community?

(f) If all of the groups have drawn males or identified male characteristics, ask them to draw or identify the characteristics of the British woman.

(g) Discuss the ways in which we develop stereotypes and the effect these have on our attitudes to female and male behaviour.

(h) Focus discussion on ideas for changing common stereotypes to be more inclusive of minority groups and females.

The family tree

Objectives:
- To develop a family tree which highlights women within the family.
- To provide a positive interpretation of women's role in the family.

Prerequisites: None.

Time needed: An introductory session of 10-15 minutes.
One week for research.
45 minutes for sharing.

What you need: A copy of the 'Family tree worksheet' (p.69), and a pen for each participant.

What you do:
(a) Hand out a copy of the worksheet to each participant.

(b) Explain that history very seldom highlights the role of women and that this activity will allow individuals and the group to explore, in their own families, the influence and background of the female members.

(c) Ask participants to take the family tree home and complete it by interviewing female members of the family.

(d) At the next session, invite participants to share what they discovered about their families.

(e) Focus discussion on the role women play, how much of women's achievements are well known and why? Are women visible in family history?

Family Tree — worksheet

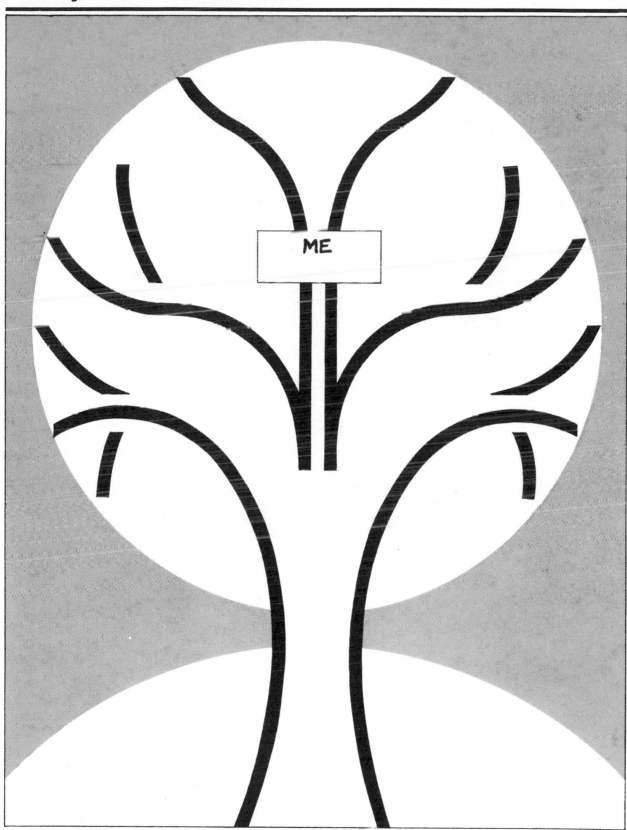

ME

Herstory

Objective: ● To collect and record an oral history from an older woman.

Prerequisites: None.

Time needed: 60 minutes to introduce the strategy and prepare a set of questions.

2-7 days to collect the woman's story.

60 minutes to share the findings.

What you need: Writing materials, and if possible, a portable tape recorder and microphone for each participant.

What you do: (a) Explain that participants are to contact a woman in their family, or a friend, who is one or two generations older than them, and is willing to be interviewed about her life, especially childhood and early adulthood.

(b) Through small group discussion and negotiation, develop a set of questions to assist the woman to remember aspects of her life story.

(c) Set a time to finish the assignment.

(d) At the next session, share the stories with the group, and put them together to form a collection of women's story tapes or papers.

Variation: The group could visit an old peoples home or pensioners club and conduct interviews. Local history societies may be able to provide photographs to act as trigger material for older people.

The man in the moon

Objectives:	● To demonstrate the power of language.
	● To show that words can exclude a large proportion of the population.
Prerequisites:	None. This activity could best be used as an introduction to the issue of sexist language.
Time needed:	45-50 minutes.
What you need:	Large sheets of flipchart paper and felt tip pens.
What you do:	(a) Provide each participant with paper and felt tip pens.
	(b) Ask each participant to quickly write or draw the first thing that they think of when a selection of the following phrases or words are read to them:

- primitive man
- man conquers space
- man overboard
- policeman
- mankind
- the man in the street
- the newsman interviewed the star
- the best man for the job
- business man of the year
- the wise men of the village

Select 3 or 4 phrases, and allow time between each for participants to finish drawing.

(c) In the large group, share the drawings or words and discuss the implications of these.

Variation:	Divide the large group into small groups of three of four participants. Give an envelope to each small group with one of the phrases or words and have each group prepare a collage to depict the phrase. Share these with the large group and discuss.

Women gossip, men talk

Objectives:
- To examine the myths and realities about female and male communication.

Prerequisites: None.

Time needed: 30 minutes.

What you need: Large sheets of flipchart paper and felt tip pens.

What you do:

(a) Ask the large group to form into small groups with 3-4 participants in each.

(b) Explain the rules of brainstorming (p.25).

(c) Half of the small groups brainstorm the words and phrases which describe women talking. The other half brainstorm the words and phrases used to describe men talking.

(d) After five minutes, ask the groups to share their lists and make two composite lists, one for women the other for men.

(e) Note any differences and similarities in the two lists and ask the group to share any other common myths about women's communication.

(f) Discuss why these myths exist and share some of the facts.

Opposite and unequal

Objectives:
- To explore the way in which words can change meaning through time.
- To examine the value given to words in female and male equivalents.

Prerequisites: Literacy skills.

Time needed: 15-20 minutes.

What you need: A thesaurus, dictionary, list of words, paper and pen for each small group.

What you do:

(a) Divide the large group into small groups of 3-4 participants and ask each group to appoint a recorder to keep notes.

(b) Provide each group with paper, pen, Thesaurus, dictionary and a list of words.

(c) Ask each group to agree on the everyday meanings of the words and then to check the dictionary for definitions and the thesaurus for synonyms.

(d) When each group has finished, ask them to share their definitions and discuss why supposedly equivalent words have different meanings.

patron	matron
master	mistress
host	hostess
waiter	waitress
Lord	Lady
actor	actress
husband	wife
landlord	landlady
bachelor	spinster
wizard	witch
call-boy	call-girl

Why can't a woman . . .?

Objectives:
- To investigate the difference in female and male communication in a mixed group.
- To discuss the myths about female communication.

Prerequisites: Some discussion on communication. 'Women gossip, men talk' (p.72) is a prerequisite activity.

Time needed: 45-50 minutes initially.

Time between sessions to observe.

45-50 minutes to process the information.

What you need: Paper and pens.

What you do: (a) Ask the participants to prepare a checklist so that they can observe a series of conversations. They could consider such things as:

Eye contact
- where do men look?
- where do women look?
- how many times do women look at the other person(s)?
- how many times do men look at the other person(s)?

Posture
- how much space do women take?
- how much space do men take?
- how and where do they sit or stand?

Tone and pitch
- what tone and pitch are used by each sex?

Amount of talk
- what length of time do women talk compared to men?
- who changes the topic?
- who interrupts and when?
- do the men talk to each other more than to the women?

Inflection
- how often do women end sentences as a question?

Words
- how many times do women use words like 'just', 'only', 'sorry'?

(b) After the participants have generated a check list, ask them to observe conversations and keep a record.

(c) At the end of a set period (no more than a week), collate the information collected and discuss the implications of the findings.

(d) Examine the lists of myths from 'Women gossip, men talk'. Ask them to compare these with their findings. What is the reality? Where do the myths originate? Do women believe the myths themselves.

(e) Focus discussion on whose interests are served by maintaining these myths.

Getting it right

Objectives:
- To provide participants with examples of non-sexist language.
- To give participants the opportunity to practise changing sexist statements into non-sexist statements.

Prerequisites: Discussion about sexist language.

Time needed: 30-45 minutes.

What you need: A copy of the worksheet (p.77) and pen for each participant.

What you do:
(a) Hand out copies of the worksheet and ask the group to divide into small groups of three.

(b) Ask each group to discuss the statements and rewrite them so that they are no longer sexist;

(c) In the large group, share the rewritten sentences and discuss the changes.

Variation: After using the worksheet, hand out some newspapers and ask the group to find examples of sexist language and statements and re-write them.

Getting it right — worksheet

Example	Alternative
a. Mary Wells is a highly successful woman advertising executive.	a. Mary Wells is a highly successful advertising executive.

b. The man in the street.

c. Peter listened patiently to the ladies' chatter.

d. The lady doctor performed the operation.

e. The man and his wife.

f. You can always pick a woman driver.

g. Mrs. Brown, mother of four, was one of the speakers at the science conference.

h. The best man for the job.

i. The pioneers moved west taking their wives and children with them.

j. John the lawyer, and an attractive blonde, arrived first at the reception.

The sins of the mothers

Objectives:
- To examine the images of women held by major religions.
- To discuss the effect that traditional religious institutions have on women's perception of themselves.

Prerequisites: Literacy skills.

Time needed: 40 minutes.

What you need: A copy of 'The sins of the mothers discussion sheet' (p.79) for each participant.

What you do:
(a) Hand out a copy of the discussion sheet to each participant and ask them to read the statements.

(b) In small groups of 3-4, ask the participants to discuss their reactions to the statements with particular reference to:
- what is being said about women in each statement;
- what effect it has on women to be seen in this way;
- is it still the case that religions see women as described in these statements?

(c) Ask the groups to recall or research positive images and statements about women from a chosen religion and share these.

(d) Discuss the role and influence of religions in forming attitudes to ourselves and others.

The sins of the mothers — discussion paper

Your wife will be like a faithful vine within your house; your children will be like olive shoots around your table. Lo, thus shall the man be blessed who fears the Lord.
(Psalm 128:3f)

And if she vowed in her husband's house, or bound her soul by a bond with an oath; . . . But when her husband makes them null and void on the day that he hears them, then whatever proceeds out of her lips concerning her vows, or concerning her pledge of herself shall not stand: her husband has made them void, and the Lord will forgive her.
(Numbers 30:10-12)

If a man give his daughter a knowledge of the Law it is as though he taught her lechery.
(Rabbi, A.D. 90)

Better to burn the Torah than to teach it to women.
(Rabbi, A.D. 90)

Attention: For the sake of the holiness and our safety we kindly request menstruating women not to enter the temple.
(Sign in a Hindu Temple)

Women are unfit matter for ordination.
(Papal statement, Jan 25, 1983)

Women who are menstruating or who have given birth within the past 40 days are not allowed to enter the mosque because they are defiled and will contaminate the holiness . . .
(Moslem law)

And God said, Let us make man in our image, after our likeness . . . So God created man in his own image . . . male and female created he them.
(Genesis 1:26-27)

I thank thee, O Lord, that thou hast not created me a woman.
(Jewish Man's Daily Prayer)

Behold, I have two daughters who have not known man; let me bring them out to you, and do to them as you please; only do nothing to these men, for they have come under the shelter of my roof.
(Genesis 19:8)

If I was . . .

Objectives:
- To explore the differences and similarities in female and male activities.
- To introduce participants to the concepts of priority setting and decision making.

Prerequisites: Literacy skills.

Time needed: 30-45 minutes.

What you need: A pen and a copy of 'If I Was . . . worksheet' (p.81) for each person.

What you do:
(a) Hand a copy of the worksheet to each person.

(b) In the left hand column, ask participants to list twelve to fifteen things that they really like to do. They may have more or less, the number is not important. Stress that the lists are personal and they will not have to share them.

(c) When the lists are completed ask them to code their lists as instructed below. Give one code at a time allowing time between each for the completion of coding.

(d) In the first column, ask the participants to write A for any activity that is done alone or P for anything that is done with other people.

In the second column, write a pound sign opposite any activity on their list that costs more than three pounds each time they do it.

In the third column, write an M against those activities that their mother would also enjoy or have enjoyed.

In the fourth column, ask them to code O against those activities that they would still do if they were a member of the opposite sex.

In the last column, put a 1 opposite the activity most enjoyed, then a 2 opposite the next most enjoyed activity and a 3 opposite the third.

(e) When the coding is completed, ask the participants to review the lists and think about some of the following questions:
- Are there any patterns?
- Were there any surprises?
- Is there anything they would like to change?
- How many activities would they still do as a member of the opposite sex?
- What activities would be added?

(f) Ask the participants to complete the sentence stems.

(g) In small groups, discuss the completed sentences.

If I was — worksheet

Things I like to do	Alone/others	£	Mother	Opposite sex	Rank

I was surprised that I ....
....
....

I learnt that I ....
....
....

If I was a member of the opposite sex I ....
....
....

Messages

Objectives:
- To recall the messages transmitted to children about women's roles.
- To provide participants with the opportunity to project into the future.
- To examine the ways in which the messages can be changed.

Prerequisites: Literacy skills.

Time needed: 45-60 minutes.

What you need: A copy of the 'Messages worksheet' (p.83) for each participant.

What you do:
(a) Hand out a copy of the worksheet to each participant and ask them to complete the sentence stems.

(b) Allow enough time for each participant to complete the worksheet and then divide the group into small groups of 3 or 4.

(c) Ask each group to discuss from their worksheets, the messages they received and what they would like to tell their daughters.

(d) In the large group, discuss the messages we receive as children and the way in which these affect our perceptions of ourselves as women.

Messages — worksheet

When I was younger, the messages I got about:

(a) *School*
from my mother ....

....

from other women such as my aunt, sister, grandmother ....

....

from my father ....

....

(b) *Work for women*
from my mother ....

....

from other women such as my aunt, sister, grandmother ....

....

from my father ....

....

(c) *Marriage and having children*
from my mother ....

....

from other women such as my aunt, sister, grandmother ....

....

from my father ....

....

(d) *The way I should look and behave*
from my mother ....

....

from other women such as my aunt, sister, grandmother ....

....

from my father ....

(e) *I wish they had told me*
my mother ....

....

other women such as my aunt, sister, grandmother ....

....

my father ....

....

(f) *If I had a daughter I would tell her* ....

....

....

(g) *I would want her to be* ....

....

....

Permission to photocopy.

Women in songs

Objective: To examine the role of women in songs.

Prerequisites: None.

Time Needed: 45-60 minutes.

What You Need: Flip chart paper and felt tip pens. Records or cassettes with songs about women. The group can be asked to bring these.

What You Do:

(a) Listen to the songs, either in a large group, or, in small groups if you have sufficient equipment and space.

(b) Discuss what the songs say about women. What sorts of images of women exist in popular music?

(c) Ask the group to make a list of the images of women.

(d) Ask groups to share their findings. Focus discussion on the reality of the images portrayed and whether or not they relate to women's lives today. Consider the options available to the women portrayed.

Variation: The participants could bring songs written and sung by women and compare them with those written and sung by men.

Background Reading

Belotti, E. G., *Little Girls*, Readers and Writers Publishing Co-op, 1975.

Sharpe, Sue, *Just like a Girl: How girls learn to be women*, Penguin, 1976.

Nicholson, Joyce, *What society does to Girls*, Virago, 1977.

Spender, Dale, *Man Made Language*, Routledge & Kegan Paul, 1980.

Hemmings, *Girls Are Powerful*, Sheba Feminist Publishers, 1982.

Root, Jane, *Pictures of Women _ Sexuality*, Pandora Books for Channel 4, 1984.

McRobbie, Angela and Nava, Mica (eds), *Gender and Generation*, Macmillan, 1984.

Dickson, Ann, *The Mirror Within*, Quartet, 1985.

Trenchard, Lorraine (ed),*Talking about young lesbians*, London Gay Teenage Group, 1984.

Warren, H. and Trenchard, Lorraine, *Something to tell you*, London Gay Teenage Group, 1984.

Resources

Adams, Carol and Laurikietis, Rae, *The Gender Trap _ Messages & Images*, Virago, 1976.

Crampton-Smith, Gillian and Curtis, Sarah, discussion material 'Sex Roles' from the 'It's Your Life' series of Thinkstrips Longmans.

Selling Pictures (Teaching Pack) BFI Publications. A useful pack of slides and photosheets to help challenge stereotypes by examining women's magazines.

Superman and the Bride, 1975. Video (45 mins) made by Thames T.V. on Sex Roles and Media Influence, Guild Sound and Vision.

Rogers, Rex and Wendy, *Men and Women*, Nelson Health Education Series, 1978.

Beecham, Yvonne et al, *Childhood: A study in socialisation*, Harrap, 1980.

A Token Gesture, 1977. Colour film (8 mins). A satirical cartoon film made for the women's programme, Canada, about the unfair treatment of women, Concord Films Council.

True Romance, 1981. Film (35 mins) useful for discussion on sex-role stereotyping and sexism, Concord Films Council Ltd.

Hamari Rangily Zindagi _ Our Colourful Lives. Video of Asian girls talking about themselves. NAYC.

A Woman's Worth

It isn't that long ago that women were bought and sold as chattels, and had no rights; they weren't allowed to own property. During times of war, work traditionally designated 'mens work' has been capably carried out by women, and history has shown that after each World War, women have been pushed out of these areas of work back into domestic and other stereotyped labour.

For many years, women fought for the principle of equal pay for equal work, and even though this principle is now embodied in legislation, in reality women still don't earn pay equal to men because of limited job opportunities and distorted employment statistics. Today women are fighting for the principle of equal opportunities, and for the implementation of positive discrimination to ensure that equality of outcome is achieved.

In this section, the strategies focus on women in employment and unemployment, including hidden unemployment; women's role in housework and the family and ways for young women to set priorities and goals for their own work in the future.

Strategies

Random words	Breaking In
Women in the workforce	Panel interviews
Division of labour brainstorm	Equal pay?
Making changes	Just a housewife
Young women and unemployment	A womans worth
Women & work	In a job I want
	Affirmative action lucky dip

Random words

Objective: ● To examine attitudes to employment and unemployment.

Prerequisites: None.

Time needed: 30 minutes.

What you need: A copy of the 'Random words worksheet', printed on both sides of a page, for each participant.

What you do:
(a) Explain to the participants that they will only have to share as much of this strategy as they choose.

(b) In the circle on one side of the worksheet, ask participants to write the word EMPLOYMENT. Quickly and without any discussion ask them to think of the words that come immediately to mind when they see or hear that word, and write them on the spokes of the wheel.

(c) Without discussion, ask them to turn the sheet over and write the word UNEMPLOYMENT in the circle and repeat the process.

(d) Ask them to reflect on the words on both sides of the sheet. What word or words do they identify as most important? Ask them to underline the word or words.

(e) By comparing both sides of the pages, ask participants to think about their attitude to employment and unemployment. At the bottom of the worksheet, ask them to complete one of the sentence stems.

(f) In small groups the participants share their sentences and discuss their attitudes to Employment and Unemployment.

Variations. Substitute the words WORK and HOUSEWORK for employment and unemployment.

Random words — worksheet

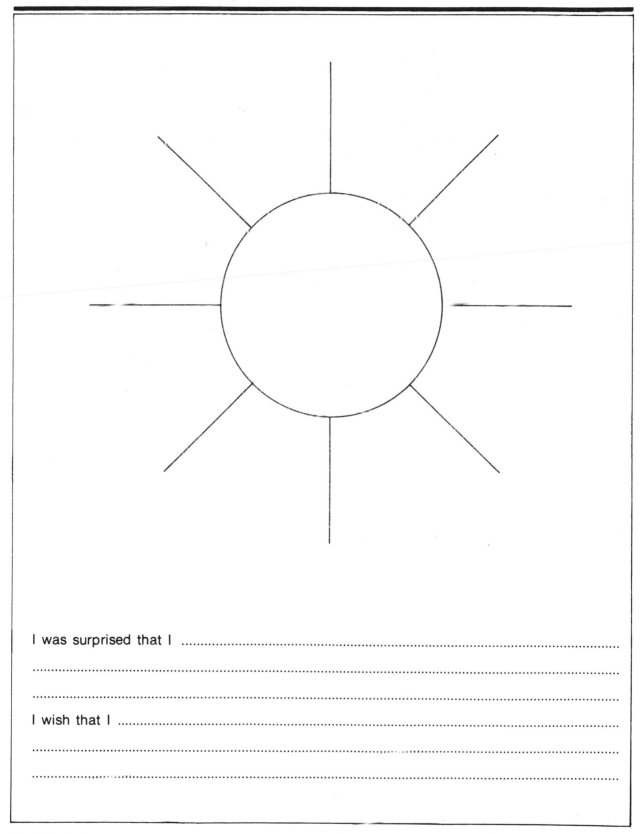

I was surprised that I ....

....

....

I wish that I ....

....

....

Women in the workforce

Objectives:
- To explore issues related to women and work.
- To raise consciousness about the facts and to dispel myths about women in the workforce.

Prerequisites: For the group leader: to have read the recommended background reading and to have the relevant facts and figures to present to the group.

Time needed: 30 minutes.

What you need: A photocopy of the relevant 'discussion sheet' (p.91) for each participant.

What you do:
(a) Divide the group into small groups of 5-6 and explain that the statements on the discussion sheets are designed to trigger discussion.

(b) Ask each participant to read the statements and to prepare a list of questions and comments.

(c) The small groups then discuss the statements using the questions as a guide. A recorder appointed by each group should write down the major points of the discussion for later sharing.

(d) Reform the total group and share the findings. Correct any misconceptions, and answer any questions as needed.

Follow-up: Explore relevant questions further by research projects, films, visits, guest speakers, reading or any other method the group may identify.

Women in the workforce — discussion sheets

One popular explanation for youth unemployment is the participation of married women in the workforce. This explanation assumes that the work women perform in the workforce, and that of young people is interchangeable. And, that if married women left, young people would step into their jobs. Married women seldom have the kind of jobs that young women would be employed in. Another implication is that married women have less right to work than others. Unfortunately, in times of recession, it is this group that is often the first to be retrenched.

Official employment figures are based on the numbers who are registered and willing to work. The incentive to register is that doing so is a prerequisite of drawing unemployment or supplementary benefit, either because they have not worked long enough to pay sufficient contributions, or because they are married and exercised their former right to opt out of the full contributions. If these women, married or not, are living with a man, they also lose their right to supplementary benefit. Having therefore no financial incentive to register as unemployed, many fail to do so!

Webb, M., The Labour Market in Reid, I. and Wormald, E., Sex Differences in Britain 1982, Grant McIntyre.

Young women who stay at home to housekeep because they are not able to find work, also contribute to this increasing number of unemployed. These women are often not encouraged to apply for benefits because their family sees their role as one centred around the house.

The nuclear family in our society is becoming more and more isolated and so relatives are less available to provide back-up support such as assisting in childcare. With the increasing numbers of women returning to the workforce (or seeking work), there is an increased demand for adequate child-care facilities.

Many women are forced to take part-time work due to the shortage of full-time jobs, therefore they are under paid and form part of the hidden unemployed. Many women claim they want part-time work so they can cope with families, etc. This may be the case, but it is difficult to be sure whether this is a real choice especially after years of socialisation and stereotyping. Although part-time work appears to be a preference for married women, it is possible it may become a permanent feature of the workforce in the future.

Although the situation is slowly changing, Trades Unions are traditionally a male domain. Everything from the way they are structured and the timing of meetings, to the way meetings are run and the issues that are seen as important, work against women being involved.

Married women make up the bulk of the hidden unemployed. Although many say that they choose to stay at home and do not want to work outside, there is also a large proportion who would seek work if they felt it was available.

Many young women assume that they will marry, have children, and stay at home for the rest of their lives, caring for and being supported by their husbands. This is simply untrue.

Trades Unions can, and should, provide collective bargaining power and protection to improve pay and working conditions for all their members.

Division of labour brainstorm

Objectives: ● To examine sex-role stereotyping in employment.

                    ● To explore some of the reasons for the sexual division of labour.

Prerequisites: None.

Time needed: 30 minutes.

What you need: Large sheets of flipchart paper, felt tip pens and a white board.

What you do: (a) In small groups of 5-6, ask half of the groups to brainstorm (p.25) all the kinds of jobs that women do, and the other half to brainstorm all the kinds of jobs that men do.

                  (b) After 10 minutes compare the lists. As the groups report to the larger group, prepare three lists which show women only jobs, men only jobs and those which appear on both lists.

                  (c) Now examine the male only list. Are there any jobs that females cannot do or never do? Why are they attributed or available only to men?

                      Do the same with the female list.

                  (d) Discuss the reasons for the stereotyping of employment and division of labour. What are the values underlying the division? How can we overcome them? What role do economics play in the division? Who benefits?

Follow up: Making changes

Making changes

Objective: ● To develop problem-solving skills.

Prerequisites: Division of labour brainstorm.

Time needed: 30 minutes.

What you need: White board or large sheets of flipchart paper.

What you do:
(a) Identify a particular problem related to the sexual division of labour from the previous stragegy. Write this at the top of the board or on a large piece of paper on the wall. Divide the sheet in half by drawing a line down the centre of the board or page.

(b) Ask the group to call out all the *positive* forces — those things in favour of bringing about positive change in the situation and list these on the right hand side.

(c) Ask them to identify all the *negative* forces — those working against change, and list these on the left hand side.

(d) Examine and discuss each of the negative forces.

How can they be changed or eliminated?

(e) Then discuss how the positive forces can be enhanced?

(f) Keep this board or sheet on display and return to it as discussion indicates in future sessions. Work on putting the positive forces into play whenever possible.

Note: This strategy can be used as a problem solving tool for a range of other subjects.

Young women and unemployment — true or false

Objective: ● To provide accurate information about young women and unemployment.

Prerequisites: This is a good introductory activity.

Time needed: 10-15 minutes.

What you need: A copy of the 'True or False Quiz' (p.96) for each participant.

What you do:
(a) Explain to the group that this is not a test.
(b) Hand a copy of the quiz to each participant and ask them to put a tick in the true or false column against each statement.
(c) Share the results and discuss why young women are more likely to be unemployed than young men.
(d) Discuss the groups of young women which are most likely to be highly represented amongst the unemployed. Why might this be?

Note: This strategy can be done as a verbal quiz with a show of hands from participants.

Answers:
a False   e True
b True   f True
c False   g True
d True

Young Women and Unemployment — True or False Quiz.

True   False

a. Young women are a majority of unemployed teenagers.

b. Unemployment rates are higher for young men than for young women.

c. Young women are far less likely than young men to enter further education.

d. Unemployed young women are more highly educated than unemployed young men

e. Young women are more likely to be part of the hidden unemployed than young men.

f. The recent growth of part-time work offers more job opportunities for women than for men.

g. Women have less choice in the type of job open to them.

Women and work

Objective: To look at some facts about women and work outside the home.

Prerequisites: Literacy skills

Time Needed: 30-45 minutes.

What You Need: A copy of the 'Women and Work' factsheet for each participant or group.

What You Do:
1. Ask small groups to read and discuss the facts and statements about women and work.
2. Ask each group to choose one which they feel particularly strongly about and ask them to present their ideas about it to the whole group.
3. Discuss the reality of women working outside the home.

Variation: Give each group one statement to discuss and present.

Women and work factsheet

One study of clerical workers demonstrated that women get 20-50% less office space than men doing roughly the same job in the same office and that the more women there were in a particular area, the lower the standard of decoration.

Benet, M., *Secretary*, Sidgwick and Jackson, 1972.

Almost 2 million women work in occupations that are almost entirely (over 90%) done by women: typists, secretaries, maids, nurses, canteen assistants, sewing machinists. Many of these 'women only' occupations give paid employment for work very similar to the tasks a woman faces at home.

CIS Report, *Women in the 80's*, 1981.

Women's jobs are notorious badly paid. In 1980, women earned, on average, only 72% as much as men.

CIS Report, *Women in the 80's*, 1981.

In most workplaces you will find there are more women at the bottom of the career structure. Men are more likely to rise to supervisory or management positions. For example, teachers have had equal pay since 1963, but more men than women reach the top of the profession. In secondary schools, 58% of all teachers on the lowest grade are women. But only 17% of all headteachers are women!

Morris, Jo, *No More Peanuts*, N.C.C.L., 1983.

Most women, whether or not they have children, do two jobs — one unpaid job at home, and one paid job outside. For women who have children, this double burden is particularly hard:

    54% of women with children under 16 are out of work.

    30% of women with children under 5 are out of work.

Working Women, T.U.C., 1983.

Women make up 86% of part-time workers. 41% of all women work less than 30 hours a week — which is how government statistics define 'part-time'. The reasons are quite clearly to do with women's unpaid work and their 'caring' role in the home. Part-time workers usually suffer from low pay, poor conditions, few promotion prospects and little job security or legal protection.

Working Women, T.U.C., 1983.

Activity rates for black women vary according to their particular background. A very high percentage of West Indian women work (74% compared to 43% of the general population) as do a high percentage of non Moslem Asian women (45%) . . . Black women tend to be in jobs such as nurses, teachers, typists and shop assistants. Black women are in the distinctly lower status jobs than their white counterparts, although the differences are not as great as between men. This reflects upon the national level of earnings of black women which is lower than that of white women.

Women in the Labour Market, T.U.C., 1983.

An analysis of black unemployment figures suggests that in times of rapidly rising unemployment black people are very vulnerable . . . There is also evidence that unemployment rates vary according to whether the person was born here or abroad and according to ethnic groups. Pakistani and Bangladeshi women appear to fare particularly badly.

Women in the Labour Market, T.U.C., 1983.

Women are half the world's population. They are a third of the official labour force they put in two-thirds of all the hours worked. They get a tenth of the world's income.

International Labour Organisation.

Breaking In

Objective:
- To plan ways for young women to break into non-traditional occupations.

Prerequisites: None.

Time needed: 35-40 minutes.

What you need: Large sheets of flipchart paper and felt tip pens.

What you do:
(a) Divide the group into small groups of 4-5.

(b) Explain the rules of brainstorming (p.25).

(c) Ask the small groups to brainstorm a list of occupations which are not considered as suitable for, or easily available to women.

(d) After five minutes, ask each group to select one occupation from their list. If possible the occupation should be one that is both difficult for women to enter and of interest to the group.

(e) Ask the groups to plan the way in which they could break into that occupation, taking into account:

- the skills or qualifications they would need;
- the location of the job and the facilities available;
- likely problems and difficulties;
- places to go for help and support;
- how Trades Unions can help.

(f) Ask the small groups to explain their strategy to the other groups. Discuss the strengths and weaknesses of each of the strategies presented.

Variation: The small group could report back by role-playing.

Panel interviews

Objectives:
- To expose participants to alternative role models.
- To explore a range of questions about women in the workforce.
- To communicate skills.

Prerequisites: Breaking in (p.100).

Time needed: 30 minutes in the first session.

Time between sessions.

60-90 minutes.

What you need: Nothing.

What you do:

(a) Explain to the group the idea of bringing together a panel of women who work in non-traditional occupations. Using the lists generated in 'Breaking In', ask them to identify some non-traditional jobs that they would like to hear more about.

(b) Ask the group to identify what they want the speakers to cover as well as time and location and format of the session.

(c) Ask for volunteers from the group to help identify and contact women to participate in the panel. This will need to be done well in advance of the session.

(d) Work with the group to develop a list of questions to ask the panel members. This will help stimulate discussion and will also ensure that the group gets the maximum from the panel

(e) On the day of the panel, set the room up for a panel discussion. Each guest should present a brief description of what she does and how she got into that position, plus any comments she may have. Follow up with questions and discussion from the group.

Follow up: At later sessions, follow-up any points that arise from the panel.

Equal pay?

Objectives:
- To identify the occupations which are seen as being for women and those which are seen as being for men.
- To compare salaries in traditionally female and male occupations.
- To increase participants' research and communication skills.
- To learn about community resources.

Prerequisites: Literacy skills.

Time needed: 10-15 minutes at the first session.

Time between sessions.

40-45 minutes at the second session.

What you need: A copy of the 'Equal pay? worksheet' (p.103) for each participant.

What you do:

(a) Hand out a copy of the worksheet to each participant.

(b) Ask them to put a tick in the female column against those occupations which are predominately female occupations.

Repeat the instruction for the male column.

(c) Discuss their responses and the differences between female and male occupations.

(d) Ask group members to select an occupation and collect the necessary information to complete the next three columns by the next session. This information can be found in careers brochures and the employment section of newspapers, the Trades Unions and professional associations.

(e) At the next session, participants share their information so that each participant has a complete chart.

(f) Use the information to draw a large bar graph which shows salary and occupation.

(g) In small groups, ask participants to discuss their findings.

Equal pay? — worksheets

Occupation	Female	Male	Salary	% of females in occupation	Qualificattions needed
Factory worker					
Taxi driver					
Airline flight attendant					
Solicitor					
Doctor					
Architect					
Vet					
Airline pilot					
Primary school teacher					
Accountant					
Engineer					
Social worker					
Town planner					
Bookkeeper					
Computer programmer					
Secretary					
Carpenter					
Nurse					
Shop assistant					
Motor mechanic					
Secondary School Headteacher					
Nursery Nurse					

Just a housewife

Objectives: ● To explore the common perceptions of housework.

● To establish the amount of time that women spend on tasks within the home.

Prerequisites: None.

Time needed: Two 45 minute sessions, 1 week apart. Individual participants complete the time charts in the week between the two sessions.

What you need: Flipchart paper and felt tip pens, *or* magazines, glue, scissors and sticky tape.

What you do: (a) Divide the group into small groups of 3-5 participants.

(b) Explain the rules of brainstorming (p.25) and ask each group to brainstorm all of the work done by women in the home.

(c) After ten minutes, ask the groups to share their lists and make a composite list.

(d) From the composite list ask the group to design a time chart (see p.120 for an example) and make a copy for each member of the group.

(e) Ask participants to enlist the help of other women in their home to keep the chart over the next week.

(f) At the next session, ask the participants to share their results, prepare a large wall chart and discuss the range of tasks which are undertaken by women in the home. Also discuss ways housework can be reallocated in the home.

Variation: Instead of the brainstorm, ask the group to make a collage which shows women's work within the home.

Just a housewife — worksheet

Time chart

Task	Mon hrs mins	Tues hrs mins	Wed hrs mins	Thurs hrs mins	Fri hrs mins	Sat hrs mins	Sun hrs mins	Total
Laundry								
Home maintenance								
Cooking								
Dishwashing								
Caring for sick								
Cleaning								
Shopping								
Gardening								
Child care								
Ironing								
Sewing								
Total								

A woman's worth

Objectives:
- To cost the work done by women in the home.
- To identify the skills and qualifications needed to do similar work outside the home.
- To increase communication skills.

Prerequisites: This would be an excellent strategy to follow 'Just a housewife' but can be done independently.

What you need: Flipchart paper and felt tip pens.

What you do:
(a) Divide the group into small groups of 3-5 participants.

(b) Explain the rules of brainstorming (p.25) and ask each group to brainstorm all of the work done by women in their home.

(c) After ten minutes, as the small groups to share their lists and form a composite list on the 'A Woman's Worth worksheet' (p107).

(d) Break the large group into new groups of 3-4 participants and allow each group to select a section of the composite list to investigate.

(e) Each group is to investigate:
- The current wages for the tasks on their list.
- The skills and qualifications needed to do those tasks outside the home.

(f) At the next session, ask the group to share their findings and discuss.

(g) If this activity is done in conjunction with 'Just a housewife', the group can actually cost the work done by women in the home during a week.

Note: Points (a) to (c) can be eliminated if following 'Just a housewife'.

A woman's worth — worksheet

Task	Skills or qualifications	Hourly Rate	Time during week hrs. mins.	Woman's worth *(calculated against hourly rate)*
e.g. Cleaning	None	£2.50	12 hours 30 mins.	£31.25
Total:				

In a job I want . . .

Objectives:
- To provide opportunity for participants to identify priorities for selecting jobs.
- To develop goal-setting and decision-making skills.

Prerequisites: Literacy skills.

Time needed: 30-40 minutes.

What you need: A copy of 'In a job I want . . . worksheet' (p.109) for each participant.

(b) Ask participants to complete section A by ranking from one to twelve what they most want in a job, using the list provided.

(c) Divide the group into small groups to discuss their rankings.

(d) Ask individuals to complete sections B and C of the worksheet.

(e) Allow time for small group discussion then ask each participant to complete section D.

In a job I want — worksheet

A   Qualities
     most wanted

1 ....

2 ....

3 ....

4 ....

5 ....

6 ....

7 ....

8 ....

9 ....

10 ....

11 ....

12 ....

   Qualities
   least wanted

> glamour, status,
> money, travel,
> challenge, freedom,
> to be my own boss,
> satisfaction, security,
> fun, friendship,
> other ....

B What sort of job(s) will provide me with my top three choices?

C What qualifications and skills would I need to get such a job(s)?

D What would I need to do if I want a job like this?

Positive action lucky dip

Objectives:
- To develop an understanding of the concept of equal opportunities, and terms used in relation to this concept.
- To have fun while learning.

Prerequisites: Literacy skills.

Time needed: 30 minutes.

What you need: The glossary of terms used (p.111), cut into sections and placed in a bowl as a lucky dip. The definition of each term.

What you do:
(a) Explain that in the lucky dip there are a number of words that are frequently used in relation to equal opportunities.

(b) A volunteer from the group draws a word out of the lucky dip and reads it to the group. Group members quickly write down the meaning of the word, or what they think it means. Remember to explain that this activity is fun, and is not a test.

(c) Individuals read out their definitions. If anyone is correct, her definition is affirmed, and put on the board in view. If no-one is correct, read out the definition and display it.

(d) Continue this process until all the words have been defined.

(e) Discuss and clarify any points as necessary.

Variation: Small groups could role-play or mime their understanding of each word, with discussion and clarification at the end of each play.

Positive action

Sexism: discrimination against women on the basis of their sex.

Sexist: an adjective describing anything which discriminates against women on the basis of their sex.

Non-sexist can apply to anything which treats or portrays women and men as equals.

Anti-sexist: actions or behaviours which consciously seek to redress the current sexist nature of our society.

Feminist: a feminist is a woman who is actively working towards the liberation of women and society based on equality for all people.

Suffragist: a person, usually female, who agitated for the vote for women around the turn of the century.

Equal rights: persons have the same rights before the law and in society.

Equal opportunity: persons are given equal chances to develop their full potential. It is not the same as equality of outcome.

Positive action: remedial action taken to correct the fact that persons have not been given equal opportunities to develop their full potential. The action is intended to bring the disadvantage up to the same level to compete on an equal basis.

Positive discrimination: action taken to correct a state where there has not been equality of outcome and there is an urgent need to have unrepresented persons included even if they are not as experienced as others.

Discrimination: making distinctions between people. In modern usage it refers to choosing people for reasons other than qualifications or ability.

Oppression: to keep inferior by coercion or injustice.

Separatist: one who chooses to live with like minded people cut off from or with minimal contact with the dominant society, e.g. women other groups.

Non-sexist language: language which includes women and does not use so called 'generic' terms, such as 'man', to include women and men.

Non-traditional jobs: jobs which have been traditionally denied to women and considered as male only occupations.

Sexual harassment: unwanted and unsolicited sexual attention, e.g. wolf-whistles, comments, touching, suggestions, pressure to have sex.

Women's liberation: a movement of individual women and women's groups struggling to change a social and economic system which is oppressive to women.

Women's movement: a broad, loose coalition of women engaged in activities to improve the status of women in society.

Reactionary: usually applied to people who react against positive policies or actions which will improve the status of women, or any oppressed group.

Patriarchy: a system or government based on male right to rule.

Background Reading

Reid, Ivan and Wormald, Eileen (eds), *Sex Differences in Britain*, Grant McIntyre, 1982.

Coote, Anna, *Equal at Work: Women in men's jobs*, Collins, 1979.

Oakley, Ann, *Subject Women*, Martin Robertson, 1981.

Spender, Dale, *Women of Ideas (and what men have done to them)*, Routledge & Kegan Paul, 1983.

Equality Now!, EOC, Overseas House, Quay Street, Manchester, M3 3HN. A free quarterly bulletin on equal opportunities.

Beale, Jenny, *Getting it together: Women as Trade Unionists*, Pluto Press, 1982.

CIS Report, *Women in the 80's*, 1981.

TUC Report, *Women in the Labour Market*, 1983.

Resources

The Impossible Dream, 1984. A film (8 mins) made for the U.N. about a fantasy world where household tasks are shared equally between women and men. Concord Films Council.

Morris, Jo, *No More Peanuts*, NCCL, 1983.

TUC Report, *Working Women*, 1983.

Working Now, Curriculum Development Support Unit. Pack of photographs and teachers booklet to help child with an understanding of non-sexist waged work.

Bitter Wages, 1984. Video (37 mins). Women and work hazards group. This film looks at women in paid work and is concerned with dangers of such areas as new technology, physical and chemical hazards, stress and racism.

Rosie the Riveter. Film (65 mins) examinining womens work in the U.S. during the 1940's. Other Cinema.

Not another training scheme. Video showing girls in non-stereotypical jobs. CFL Vision.

What are you really made of? Video (17 mins). Interviews with women in non-stereotypical jobs. EOC.

What's a girl like you? Video (23 mins) looks at women engineers. EOC.

Liberating Learning

In school we learn more than what is in the curriculum. The hidden curriculum provides more powerful, if subtle messages about class, race and sex. In school books, the Janet and John stereotypes confirm our developing attitudes. Arithmetic texts pose appropriate problems. Janet has three pies while John has three rockets. The lessons are learnt. Janet watches the stoves while John looks to the stars.

This learning is not confined to school; our education about who we are and what we can become comes from a wide range of sources both formal and informal. This section raises issues about schools and the media as two important educational institutions. It also explores the ways in which we learn from experience and relationships, as well as lessons from the past, and how the experience and achievements of women are excluded from our formal education.

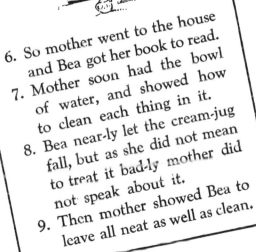

6. So mother went to the house and Bea got her book to read.

7. Mother soon had the bowl of water, and showed how to clean each thing in it.

8. Bea near-ly let the cream-jug fall, but as she did not mean to treat it bad-ly mother did not speak about it.

9. Then mother showed Bea to leave all neat as well as clean.

Strategies
Guiding lights
The ideal woman — the ideal man
Women in the media
The womens pages
What girls like — what boys like
That's what I saw on TV
School days
Text books
I didn't know she existed
Famous women in history

Guiding lights

Objectives:
- To provide opportunities for participants to identify any important people in their lives who have played the role of mentor.
- To assist identification of learning which has taken place from association with mentors.

Prerequisites: Literacy skills.

Time needed: 30-45 minutes.

What you need: A copy of the 'Guiding lights worksheet' (p.115) for each participant.

What you do:

(a) Hand out copies of the worksheet and explain that although education and learning are often only associated with schooling, this strategy will provide opportunities to explore learning in a broader context.

(b) On the lifeline, ask participants to mark in their year of birth, and their present age next to the appropriate place.

(c) Ask participants to think about people: friends or adults, who have influenced them or from whom they have learned meaningful or important lessons. Next to the age they were when they met or were influenced by that person, have them write in the person's name or initials, or use a code to indicate who she or he was.

(d) Next to the name, ask them to note down what influence that person had and what lesson they learned as a result of their association.

(e) When they are finished, ask participants to complete the sentence stems at the foot of their worksheet.

(f) Share the sentence stems and any observations or learnings in small groups of 3-4. Focus discussion on the kinds of learning, their relevance to life and whether participants had thought about these experiences as learning before.

(g) In the total group, explain the meaning and concept of 'mentor', and discuss the relevance and importance of mentors in women's lives.

Guiding lights — worksheet

Date of birth 19................

Date today 19.................

My most important lesson(s) ....

....

....

....

....

I was surprised that ....

....

....

On reflection I think that ....

....

....

The ideal woman — the ideal man

Objective:
- To explore the messages that the print media conveys about women and men.

Prerequisites: None.

Time needed: 50 minutes.

What you need: Large sheets of flipchart paper, an assortment of magazines, scissors, glue and sticky tape.

What you do:
(a) Divide the large group into groups of 3-4.

(b) Provide each group with a large sheet of paper, magazines, scissors, glue and sticky tape.

(c) Ask half of the groups to make a collage to depict the media's representation of the ideal woman. Ask the other half to do the same for the ideal man.

(d) Display the completed collages and ask the groups to explain the predominant images they found the media presented.

(e) Discussion points could include the ways in which the media creates these images; the realism of the images; the effect of the images on individuals.

Variations:
1. Ask the small groups to make a collage that depicts what *society* says about the ideal woman and the ideal man.

2. If the group is culturally homogeneous, small groups can be assigned, or choose another culture or ethnic group to research.

3. Individuals or small groups prepare a collage to depict their ideal for themselves. This can then be compared with one of the above themes.

That's what the papers say

Objective:
- To demonstrate the way the media judges women's achievements by standards different to those of men.

Prerequisites: None.

Time needed: 50 minutes.

What you need: Newspapers, magazines, journals, scissors, glue and flipchart paper.

What you do:
(a) Divide the large group into small groups of 3-5.

(b) Provide each group with magazines, newspapers, glue, etc.

(c) Have each group read through the papers and cut out any articles or stories which demonstrate a difference in the way women and men are reported.
- generalisations, e.g. mother-in-law-jokes
- references to appearance and age
- omissions of women's achievement
- reference to marital status
- occupational status

(d) Make a collage of these articles and ask each group to report their findings to the large group.

(e) Focus discussion on the differences in the way in which women and men are portrayed by the media.

Variation:
1 Using maths or science text books ask participants to look for the differences in which women and men are portrayed.
- how far women travel
- how far men travel
- what work women do
- what work men do
- how much money women spend
- how much money men spend.

2 Using newspapers and magazines ask the group to identify stories and articles written by women. Compare the number, length and content with those written by men.

Women in the media

Objectives:
- To explore a variety of issues related to the portrayal of women in the media.
- To raise awareness about these portrayals, and to explore ways to change them.

Prerequisites: For the group leader: to have read the recommended background reading and to have the relevant information ready to present to the group. Literacy skills.

Time needed: 30 minutes.

What you need: A photocopy of the relevant discussion sheet for each participant.

What you do:
    (a) Divide the group into small groups of 5-6 and explain that the statements on the discussion sheets are designed to trigger discussion.

    (b) Ask each participant to read the statements and to prepare a list of questions and comments.

    (c) The small groups then discuss the statements using the questions as a guide. A recorder appointed by each group should write down the major points of discussion for later sharing.

    (d) Reform the total group and share the findings. Correct any misconceptions and answer any questions as needed.

Follow up: Explore relevant questions further by research projects, films, visits, guest speakers, reading or any other method the group may identify.

Women in the media — discussion sheet

Television, newspapers and radio are the media that reach the greatest number of people. Unfortunately, they often show an unrealistic image of people. This image tends to be restrictive and repetitive. Women are frequently shown as housewives and mothers and almost always centred around the home with no other personal needs or interests. In reality women are often members of the workforce, which generally doesn't fit the media stereotype. However, when a woman is portrayed by the media as a member of the workforce, it is more than likely that she is working in a non-decision making capacity and is usually helping a man or men and hence fulfils the stereotype of a subordinate or dependent person.

Women have consistently objected to advertisements which degrade or insult women. The cumulative effect of these advertisements is to present women as stupid, incomplete and sex objects. Women's bodies have sold everything from cars to cigarettes. Women are particularly annoyed to see advertisements which not only show them in a domestic role at home but needing someone else to tell them how to do the housework properly.

'Women's pages' in newspapers are almost exclusively concerned with appearances, fashion, cooking and childcare.

The women's pages

Objective: ● To analyse the intent of news directed at women and the implicit messages in the content, and style of presentation.

Prerequisites: Literacy skills.

Time needed: 45 minutes.

What you need: Several different newspapers.

What you do: (a) In groups of 3, ask participants to read through the papers noting and marking on the page articles that seem to be of particular relevance to women.

(b) Ask them to look at the space allowed and the position in the paper (which page, what part of the page) and keep a record of any trends.

(c) Next ask them to read the articles and discuss the subject matter. It is imporant to record any observations they make.

(d) Re-form the total group, and ask small groups to share their findings.

(e) Discuss any trends and observations that emerge. What does the analysis say about the position of women? Are women really only interested in the types of news presented as women's news? What is the difference between what is presented as news and women's news.

Follow-up: A woman newspaper reporter could be brought in as a resource person to the group to discuss the status of women in journalism, and ways of working on the media to change their attitudes towards women.

Variation: Television programmes aimed at women could be examined in a similar way.

What girls like — what boys like

Objectives:
- To determine differences in female and male preferences to television programmes.
- To explore how the media portrays females and males, and how these portrayals effect young people's perceptions of the roles of women and men.

Prerequisites: None.

Time needed: 30 minutes at the first session.

Time between sessions.

45 minutes at the second session.

What you need: Flipchart paper and felt tip pens.

What you do:
(a) Explain that small groups are going to conduct a survey into the differences or similarities between girls and boys television viewing preferences, and the possible effects these programmes have on their perceptions of female and male roles.

(b) In small groups of 5-6, ask participants to list all the questions they might ask people to find out about their preferences, the reasons why they like particular programmes, and whether they see the characters in these programmes as realistic or admirable.

(c) Re-join the group and work together to discuss, evaluate, and prioritise the lists until a list of questions is developed to be used as a questionnaire for the survey.

(d) During an agreed period of time between sessions, participants carry out the survey in pairs.

(e) At the next session, participants share the results of their surveys. As each pair reports back, tabulate the results so that an overall picture emerges.

(f) Discussion should focus on any similarities and differences and the reasons why they exist. Explore what these preferences say about media portrayals of women and men, how realistic they are and what we learn from these programmes about being female and male.

Variation: Survey the amount of time spent watching TV by girls and boys. This could be done separately or combined with 'What girls like — what boys like'.

That's what I saw on TV

Objectives:
- To examine the way in which women are portrayed on television.
- To discuss the accuracy of the portrayal.

Prerequisites: None.

Time needed:
5 minutes at the first session.

2 days to collect the information.

45-60 minutes to discuss the results.

What you need: A copy of the 'That's what I saw on TV worksheet' for each participant.

What you do:
(a) At the end of a session, hand each participant a copy of the worksheet and ask them to watch two or three television programmes during the following days. Fill in each programme and complete the sentence stems.

(b) At the next session, ask the participants to share their findings and their reactions and develop a composite list of women characters.

(c) In small groups, discuss the way in which the media portrays women and whether this is an accurate representation.

(d) Discuss who controls the media and why they present women this way.

That's what I saw on TV — worksheet

Title of programme or advertisement

Description and/or name of character

Occupation of character

I was surprised that . . . .

. . . .

Women in the media are . . . .

. . . .

The media should . . . .

School days

Objectives: ● To trigger discussion about girls' schooling experience.

● To generate questions and comments on schooling.

Prerequisites: For the group leader: to have read the essential background reading and to have the relevant facts and figures to present to the group.

Time needed: 30 minutes.

What you need: A photocopy of the discussion sheet for each participant.

What you do: (a) Divide the group into small groups of 5 or 6 and explain that the statements on the discussion sheet are designed to trigger discussion.

(b) Ask each participant to read the statements and prepare a list of questions and comments.

(c) The small groups then discuss the statements using the questions as a guide. A recorder appointed by each group, should write down major points of the discussion for later sharing.

(d) Reform the total group and share the findings. Correct any misconceptions, and answer any questions as needed.

Follow up: Explore relevant questions further by research projects, films, visits, guest speakers, reading or any other method the group may identify.

School days — discussion sheet

Education
- 'Teachers spend about two thirds of their classroom interaction time with boys, and boys perform about two thirds of the student talk.'[1]

- '... teachers tend to know a great deal more about the boys they teach including details and characteristics. In contrast, girls are often treated as an undifferentiated group.'[1]

- 'The majority of teachers (of both sexes) preferred to teach boys, even though many stated it was easier to teach girls.'[1]

- 'Boys appear to have more space made available to them, both inside the classroom and outside (for example in corridors and playgrounds). There is evidence that more money is spent on the education of boys from craft to science and sporting facilities.'[1]

- 'Women don't talk as much as men in mixed company and girls don't talk as much as boys in mixed classrooms.'[2]

- 'Girls are no longer completely excluded from science education as a matter of principle, but all too often domestic subjects are considered to be the most suitable preparation for girls' assigned roles of housewife and mother.'[3]

[1] Dale Spender, 'The Role of Teachers — What Choices Do They Have', a paper prepared for the Council for Cultural Co-operation, Norway, 1981.
[2] Dale Spender, 'Talking Class' *in* 'Learning to Lose', 1980.
[3] L. Curran, 'Science Education: Did she drop out or was she pushed?' *in* 'Alice through the Microscope', 1980.

Text Books

Objective: ● To examine the message conveyed in text books about the roles and capabilities of females and males.

Prerequisites: None.

Time needed: 30 minutes in the first session for introduction.

Time between sessions.

45-60 minutes for the second session.

What you need: A range of school text books.

Flipchart paper and felt tip pens (session 2).

What you do: (a) At the end of a session, explain that messages are often conveyed through educational materials without ever being openly stated, for example in text books.

(b) Ask the participants to form groups of 3, and for each group to select 3 school text books from any level — primary or secondary.

During the period between this and the next session, the group is to count the number of times females are mentioned and the number of times males are mentioned in the text books. This not only includes women and men, but characters who are female or male. Also to examine the kind of activities they are involved in, and the roles they play. This information is to be documented on a chart using large sheets of paper.

(c) At the next session, ask each small group to share their findings with the group.

(d) Discuss the findings; were they surprising? What kind of messages do they give about the capabilities of women and men? Also discuss how these messages can be countered, and ways that this can be achieved.

I didn't know she existed

Objectives:
- To provide positive female role models.
- To increase participants' awareness of women's role in history.

Prerequisites: None.

Time needed: 5 minutes to introduce the activity.

2-7 days to research the subject.

45-60 minutes to present the findings.

What you need: Envelopes containing a slip of paper with the name of one of the women listed below printed on it. You will need one envelope for each pair.

What you do:

(a) At the end of a session, divide the group into pairs and let each pair select a sealed envelope.

(b) Ask each pair to collect information before the next session, on the woman specified in their envelope.

(c) At the next session, ask each pair to present the information on their woman's history.

(d) Discuss the role played by these women in history. Were the participants aware of their existence? Why are such women not given prominence in history books—

Mary Seacole	Suzanne Valadon
Amy Johnson	Mary Ann Evans
Rosalind Franklin	Gwen John
Catherine L. Green	Mary Shelley
Elizabeth Garrett Anderson	Mary Somerville
Caroline Haslett	Ruth Benedict
Dorothy Hodgkin	Elizabeth Blackwell
Barbara McIntock	Emma Goldmann

Famous women in history

Objectives:
- To explore the roles played by women and men in history.
- To demonstrate that recorded history is male biased.

Prerequisites: Literacy skills.

Time needed: 50-60 minutes.

What you need: A copy of the worksheet and a pen for each participant.

What you do:
(a) Divide the group into groups of 3-4.

(b) Hand a copy of the worksheet to each participant.

(c) Ask each small group to work together to find names of women and men to fit each category.

(d) When each group has filled in as many names as they can ask the groups to share with each other.

(e) If there are still blanks, the groups could undertake research between sessions and report to the next session.

(f) Discuss how easy or difficult it was to find names to fit each category and why.

Variation: For a group without literacy skills, this activity can be conducted as a quiz.

Famous women in history — worksheet

Women		Men
	Artists	
	Athletes	
	Aviators	
	Composers	
	Explorers	
	Hereditary leaders	
	Lovers	
	Military leaders	
	Musicians	
	National leaders	
	Novelists	
	Pirates	
	Poets	
	Religious leaders	
	Scientists	
	Tennis Players	
	Villains	

Background Reading

Chamberlain, Mary, *Fenwomen: A portrait of women in an English Village*, Virago, 1975.

Rowbotham, Sheila, *Hidden from History*, Pluto Press, 1973.

Heron, Liz (ed), *Truth, Dare or Promise: Girls growing up in the fifties*, Virago, 1985.

London Feminist History Group, *The Sexual Dynamics of History*, Pluto, 1983.

Pember Reeves, Maud, *Round About a Pound a Week*, Virago, 1979.

Goffman, Erving, *Gender Advertisements*, Macmillan, 1979.

Spender, Dale, *Man Made Language*, RKP, 1980.

Shorter, Edward, *A History of Women's Bodies*, Pelican Books, 1984.

Dixon, Bob, *Catching them young: Sex race and class in children's fiction*, Pluto, 1977.

Spender, Dale, *Invisible Women: The schooling scandal*, Writers and Readers Publishing Co-operative, 1982.

Stinton, Judith (ed), *Racism and Sexism in Childrens Books*, Writers and Readers Publishing Co-operative, 1979.

Spender, Dale and Sarah, Elizabeth, *Leaving to Lose — Sexism and Education*, The Womens Press, 1980.

Whyte, Judith, *Beyond the Wendy House*, Longman for Schools Council, 1980.

Stones, Rosemary, *Pour out the cocoa Janet*, Longmans for Schools Council, 1983.

Whyld, Janie (ed), *Sexism in the secondary curriculum*, Harper & Row, 1983.

Brighton Women & Science Group, *Alice through the microscope*, Virago, 1980.

Hartman, Mary and Banner, Lois W., *Clio's Consciousness Raised: New perspectives on the history of women*, Harper & Row, 1974.

Harding, Jan, *Switched off: The Science Education of Girls*, Longmans for Schools Council, 1983.

Resources

Adams, Carol and Laurikietis, Rae, *Gender Trap: Education and Work*, Virago, 1980.

Well Being and Being Well

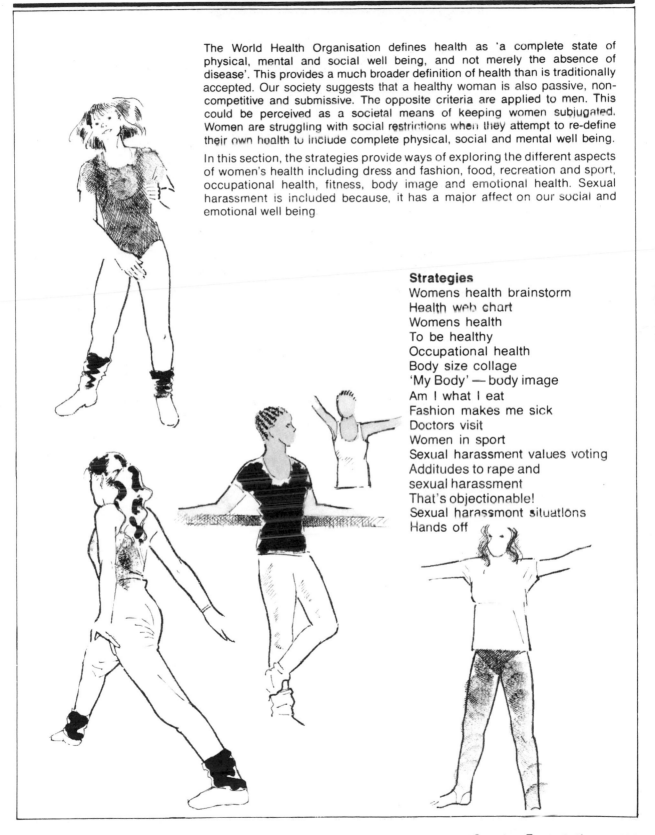

The World Health Organisation defines health as 'a complete state of physical, mental and social well being, and not merely the absence of disease'. This provides a much broader definition of health than is traditionally accepted. Our society suggests that a healthy woman is also passive, non-competitive and submissive. The opposite criteria are applied to men. This could be perceived as a societal means of keeping women subjugated. Women are struggling with social restrictions when they attempt to re-define their own health to include complete physical, social and mental well being.

In this section, the strategies provide ways of exploring the different aspects of women's health including dress and fashion, food, recreation and sport, occupational health, fitness, body image and emotional health. Sexual harassment is included because, it has a major affect on our social and emotional well being.

Strategies
Womens health brainstorm
Health web chart
Womens health
To be healthy
Occupational health
Body size collage
'My Body' — body image
Am I what I eat
Fashion makes me sick
Doctors visit
Women in sport
Sexual harassment values voting
Additudes to rape and
sexual harassment
That's objectionable!
Sexual harassmont situations
Hands off

Women's health brainstorm

Objectives:
- To identify a range of women's health issues.
- To generate a list of women's health issues for discussion.

Prerequisites: None.

Time needed: 20 minutes.

What you need. Large sheets of flipchart paper and felt tip pens.

What you do:
(a) Explain the rules of brainstorming (p.25).

(b) Ask the group to brainstorm all the words they can think of when they hear the words women's health.

(c) At the end of the designated time, ask participants to go over the lists and discuss each point. Develop a code system to identify areas of physical, social and emotional health, and to identify any issues specific to women.

(d) Discuss the contents of the lists. Do any trends emerge? What messages do the lists convey about women's health?

(e) Keep these lists, if possible on display, for future reference.

Health web chart

Objective: ● To identify the social, political and economic factors which contribute to women's ill health.

Prerequisites: Women's health brainstorm (p.132).

Time needed: 60 minutes.

What you need: A large sheet of flipchart paper and felt tip pens.

What you do:
(a) Select a health issue from the list generated in the 'womens health brainstorm', and write this in the centre of a large sheet of paper.

(b) On another sheet of paper, list all the related and contributing factors.

(c) When this list is complete, write them on the large sheet and, using a different coloured pen, interlink the different factors, as they relate to each other.

(d) A web will start to form and you will notice that the lines connect more often at certain points. These points indicate significant contributing factors, and are a good point to start from when learning about or working towards changing the situation.

(e) Identify whether these factors are social, political or economic, and develop potential change strategies.

(f) Keep the web chart on display and add to it whenever it is appropriate.

Women's health

Objectives:
- To explore a range of issues related to women's health.
- To provide accurate information about those issues.

Prerequisites: For the worker: to have read the essential background reading and to have the relevant facts and figures to present to the group.

Time needed: 30 minutes.

What you need: A photocopy of the 'Women's health discussion sheet' for each participant.

What you do:

(a) Divide the group into small groups of 5-6 and explain that the statements on the discussion sheet are designed to trigger discussion.

(b) Ask each participant to read the statements and to prepare a list of questions and comments.

(c) The small groups then discuss the statements using the questions as a guide. A recorder appointed by each group should keep the major points of the discussion for later sharing.

(d) Reform the total group and share the findings. Correct any misconceptions, and answer any questions as needed.

Follow up: Explore relevant questions further by using research projects, films, visits, guest speakers, reading or any other method the group may identify.

Women's health — discussion sheet

The World Health Organisation (W.H.O.) defines health as '. . . a state of complete physical, mental and social well-being, and not merely the absence of disease or infirmity'.	What factors prevent most women reaching the point where they can join in recreational activities?
Generally speaking women visit doctors as patients more frequently than men. This can be partly attributed to the fact that women take children and elderly relatives to the doctor.	Girls are known to be stronger at birth than boys, and it is generally recognised that women have greater resistance to extremes of temperature than men. They are less likely to suffer from hyperthermia (exposure). Women have better resistance to pain and have the inbuilt capacity to withstand the stress of childbirth.
Perhaps the most commonly abused drugs are alcohol and tobacco, followed by the over-the-counter and prescription drugs. Illegal drug use is a fairly small proportion of the overall drug problem.	The menstrual cycle has often been used as a weapon against women, yet it has been proved that almost all women are capable of normal activities (including vigorous sport) despite any discomfort at this time.
Smoking is increasing quite considerably amongst young people and especially amongst young women. A likely reason for this is the tobacco industry's campaign aimed at young people and their use of the changing role of women in society towards sexual equality.	Quite often, girls are actually bigger and stronger than boys of the same age, so there seems little logic for excluding them from the more vigorous sports.
Working environments can also contribute to poor health. Exposure to excessive noises can cause problems with hearing; bad light and having to read fine print can create sight problems; standing all day can cause varicose veins and poor ventilation can create respiratory problems.	

To be healthy . . .

Objectives:
- To explore different attitudes to health for females and males.
- To examine stereotypes.

Prerequisites: Literacy skills (for groups with limited literacy skills, see Variation 1 below).

Time needed: 45-60 minutes.

What you need: A copy of the 'To be healthy worksheets' (pp.137–138) for each participant.

What you do:

(a) Fold the worksheet on the dotted line. Hand out worksheet 1 to each participant.

Ask them individually, and without discussion, to complete the continuum for females and then turn the page and complete the continuum for males.

(b) Ask the participants to put the first sheet to one side and hand out worksheet 2 with the adult continuum and sentence stems. Ask each participant to complete the adult continuum.

(c) When participants have completed all three continuums, ask them to compare the three.

Explain that: if all the scores on the female continuum are on the right hand side and their scores for males on the left hand side, then they have a stereotyped attitude to female and male behaviour. If they have also scored the healthy adult on the left hand side of the page then they see females as being other than adult and healthy.

(d) Ask each participant to complete the sentence stems.

(e) Discuss the activity, with particular emphasis on stereotyped attitudes towards females, males in our society and the implications for women.

Variation 1: For a group with limited literacy skills, this strategy can be done by drawing the continuums on white boards or flip charts and asking participants to call the number while the worker marks them on the continuums.

Variation 2: The group can be divided into three smaller groups with each of them completing one of the continuums and then comparing.

To be healthy — worksheet 1

Female:

The healthy female is:

	1	2	3	4	5	
Aggressive						Non aggressive
Independent						Dependent
Unemotional						Emotional
Rational						Irrational
Dominant						Submissive
Non excitable						Excitable
Competitive						Non competitive
Not easily hurt						Easily hurt
Adventurous						Cautious
Leader						Follower
Not appearance oriented						Appearance oriented

Fold here

Male:

The healthy male is:

	1	2	3	4	5	
Aggressive						Non aggressive
Independent						Dependent
Unemotional						Emotional
Rational						Irrational
Dominant						Submissive
Non excitable						Excitable
Competitive						Non competitive
Not easily hurt						Easily hurt
Adventurous						Cautious
Leader						Follower
Not appearance oriented						Appearance oriented

To be healthy — worksheet 2

Adult:

The healthy adult is:

	1	2	3	4	5	
Aggressive	....					Non aggressive
Independent	....					Dependent
Unemotional	....					Emotional
Rational	....					Irrational
Dominant	....					Submissive
Non excitable	....					Excitable
Competitive	....					Non competitive
Not easily hurt	....					Easily hurt
Adventurous	....					Cautious
Leader	....					Follower
Not appearance oriented	....					Appearance oriented

Fold here   ....

On my lists females, males and adults are ....

....

I was surprised that ....

....

I learned that I ....

....

I would like to be able to ....

....

Occupational health

Objective: ● to explore work related health issues as they affect women.

Prerequisites: None.

Time needed: 15 minutes at the end of a session
Time between sessions
40-60 minutes in the final session.

What you need: Nothing.

What you do:

(a) At the end of a session, explain the concept of occupational health to the group.

(b) Divide the group into pairs and assign each group a type of occupation to research.

(c) Participants are to visit places of work, contact resource agencies or Trades Unions to research the kinds of work-related health problems experienced by workers in that particular occupation.

(d) Ask participants to prepare a presentation to the group to explain their findings at the next session. They can use any kind of presentation technique.

(e) At the next session, participants report their findings.

(f) Discuss any general health problems, and any specific to particular occupations. Focus on ways of changing these problems, safety and protective measures, and any groups or organisations working in prevention, and their role.

Some suggested occupations:

Typist	Nurse
Clerical workers	Word processing operators
Shop assistant	Factory workers (different areas)
Domestic workers	
Nursery Assistant	

Body size collage

Objectives:
- To examine how womens bodies are portrayed by the media.
- To discuss how media images influence women's self perception.

Prerequisites: None.

Time needed: 45 minutes.

What you need: Magazines, glue, scissors, pens, flipchart paper and sticky tape.

What you do:
(a) Ask small groups of 4-6 to compile a collage on the way women are portrayed in magazines. Have one group look for young women, one for middle aged and one for older women. In different parts of each collage, depict women who are very slim, average and over-weight.

(b) When the collages are completed, share them in the total group and look for any trends in images that are projected. Does body size influence how women are portrayed? Are women stereotyped according to their size? Does this vary with age?

(c) In discussion, compare the media findings to reality, how often are women really as they are portrayed in the magazines. How do these influence participants' perceptions of themselves?

Follow up: ' 'My Body' — body image' could be a useful follow-up strategy.

Variations: This activity can be done by watching TV and keeping a diary.

'My body' — body image

Objectives:
- To help participants clarify what is important to them about their bodies and appearance.
- To build confidence and practise assertive communication.

Prerequisites: This is not a suitable activity when beginning work with a particular group. It is best conducted after some work on communication and assertiveness.

Time needed: 30 minutes.

What you need: ' 'My Body' worksheet' (p.142) for each participant.

What you do:
(a) On the worksheet, have participants make a list of 13 things about their bodies that they like.

(b) In the space provided, ask them to write the 3 they would like to change or do without.

(c) Next ask them to fill in the three things that are most important about their body.

(d) Ask participants to complete the sentence stem.

(e) In groups of 3, ask participants to share what they like best about their body. Ensure that they make their statements assertively and confidently. Continue until every participant feels confident about making their statements.

(f) In the large group, discuss the activity and how participants felt making positive statements about themselves.

'My body' — worksheet

Things I like about my body:

1 ....

2 ....

3 ....

4 ....

5 ....

6 ....

7 ....

8 ....

9 ....

10 ....

11 ....

12 ....

What I would like to change or do without:

1 ....

2 ....

3 ....

The things that are most important:

1 ....

2 ....

3 ....

What I like best about my body is: ....

....

....

Am I what I eat?

Objectives:
- To provide an opportunity for participants to learn about what constitutes a healthy diet.
- To gain information about community resources.
- To develop investigative skills.

Prerequisites: None.

Time needed: 15 minutes at the end of a session.

Time between sessions.

50-60 minutes.

What you need: Nothing.

What you do:

(a) At the end of a session, ask each participant to keep a record of what she eats during the next week, noting what they eat at each meal or snack, and the brands/types of any processed foods eaten.

(b) Divide the group into 3 groups and set an assignment for each.

Group 1 Contact the local Health Education Unit (address in 'phone book) for the Health Education Authority leaflets on healthy eating. Try and make a composite list of what should be included in the daily diet. Does the information vary from leaflet to leaflet?

Group 2 Make a list of all the commercial and processed foods, and explore these brands and their additives. How many labels do not have the ingredients listed? Contact companies and find out the contents and why they are not listed.

Group 3 Your local Health Education Unit or library will be able to provide you with a list of additives and their effects. Present these on a chart.

(c) At the next session, ask the group to present their findings and compare these with the individual records. Discuss who controls the food we eat, what influences our food intake and how easy or difficult it is to have a healthy diet.

Fashion makes me sick

Objective:
● To examine clothing fashions, how they change and their effects of womens health.

Prerequisites: None.

Time needed:
10 minutes at the first session.
Time between sessions.
60 minutes.

What you need: Nothing.

What you do:
(a) At the end of a session, ask the participants in groups of 4-5 to research during the next week, clothing fashions for a particular 10 or 20 year period in the last 100 years. Different groups take different periods.

(b) At the next session, each small group presents their findings for the era they have chose. They can use photos and drawings to illustrate their findings.

(c) At the end of each presentation, ask the whole group to identify styles that distort the body, that emphasise or de-emphasise certain body characteristics or that represent a change from another era. Keep these lists for later reference.

(d) After all the presentations, compare female and male fashions, and ask which are more restricting. Discuss the effects on women's personal image, and on their health. Are corsets, high heeled shoes or tight jeans healthy? What do changing fashions say to women about their bodies? Do women feel comfortable with their bodies, or do they try to change them? What effect does this have on women's image of themselves? Who controls fashion? What choices do females have?

(e) Ask the group to design and discuss comfortable and healthy clothing.

Doctor's visit

Objectives:
- To develop a list of strategies to assert your rights when visiting a doctor.
- To practise techniques for dealing with the medical profession.

Prerequisites: None.

Time needed: 60-90 minutes.

What you need: Nothing.

What you do:

(a) Ask the group to brainstorm (p 25) and develop a list of strategies for when they visit the doctor.

(b) Divide the group into pairs and have them work out what they expect and what would need to happen for them to get what they expect from a doctor's visit.

(c) Form the pairs into groups of 6. In these small groups, pairs can share their ideas and each group then works on developing role-plays to present to the total group. After each role play, be sure to de-brief the players.

(d) At the end of all the role-plays, discuss the techniques suggested, how well they would work and any additions or modifications. Suggest that participants try out the suggestions on their next visit to the doctor.

(e) As a result of the brainstorm, discussion and role plays, develop a *List of Strategies*. Keep this on display for future reference.

Variation: Substitute a visit to a hospital, clinic, school or occupational nurse.

Women in sport

Objective: ● To examine perceptions of women in sport.

Prerequisites: None.

Time needed: 25-30 minutes.

What you need: Flipchart paper and felt tip pens.

What you do:
(a) Divide the groups into small groups of 4-5, and ask half of the groups to brainstorm (p.25) all the sports that women can play and the other half to brainstorm all the sports that men can play.

(b) After 10 minutes, compare the lists. As the groups are reporting back, prepare 3 composite lists; one for women and men, one for women only and one for men only. Compare the female and male only lists and discuss why these are different. Are there some sports that women cannot play? Why? Are more sports considered appropriate for men than for women.

(c) Discuss the effect that sex-role stereotyping in sport can have on a woman's health.

Sexual harassment — values voting

Objective: ● To explore common attitudes towards sexual harassment.

Prerequisites: None.

Time needed: 10 minutes.

What you need: Nothing.

What you do: (a) Explain the hand signals.

(b) Explain that you will read out a statement (see below) and that individuals should respond quickly, without allowing time to think or debate, with the hand signals.

(c) Read the questions. It is useful for the worker to participate also, but delay your vote so as not to influence the participants' votes.

(d) In small groups, discuss community attitudes to sexual harassment.

Note: Four to six statements are usually enough for one session. Design more statements to suit the objectives of the session, on any subject.

Statements:

1 The way girls dress these days, they are asking for trouble.

2 Women use charges of sexual harassment as a way of getting back at a man with whom they are angry.

3 Women should ignore sexual harassment when it occurs.

4 Women who object to having their bottom pinched can't take a joke.

5 Women harass men too.

6 Sexual harassment is a form of sexual discrimination.

7 It's really a compliment to have someone whistle at you in the street.

Attitudes to rape and sexual harassment

Objective:	● To discuss attitudes to rape and sexual harassment.
Prerequisites:	None.
Time needed:	45 minutes.
What you need:	A copy of the 'Attitudes to rape and sexual harassment discussion sheet' (p.149) for each participant.
What you do:	(a) Ask the participants to form into small groups.
	(b) Hand out a copy of the discussion sheet to each group.
	(c) Ask the groups to discuss the statements on the discussion sheet and the following questions: What do the statements say about the way in which rape and violence is viewed in our society? Why do we have these attitudes? What would the attitude be if it was men and not women who were raped.

Attitudes to rape and sexual harassment — discussion sheet

Ms. White who was hospitalized from three days after she was attacked and raped by an apparent Good Samaritan, was asked by a male psychiatrist at the hospital, 'Haven't you really been rushing towards this very thing all your life?' and then returning home from the hospital she was asked angrily by her husband 'If that's what you wanted why didn't you come to me?'
Diana Russell 'Rape and the Masculine Mystique' in Elizabeth Whitlegg et al. The Changing Experience of Women, Martin Robertson.

You may have noticed that a man by himself tends to stop at an encouraging wink or a cheeky remark, nothing very outrageous. It is usually only when they're together that men try to outdo each other with the crudest comments. They feel the need to 'prove' that they are men, particularly to each other. They're supposed to see women as good for one thing only and to put them down. One way of proving all this is to do it loudly and in public.
Carol Adams and Rae Laurikietis, 'The Gender Trap', Book 2, Sex & Marriage.

Britain:
Twenty-five percent of all violent crime is wife assault. As unemployed men spend more time around the house, it is likely that more and more women will be battered at home. 1978 estimates show that only one refuge was available for every 60,000 battered women.
'Women in the 80's', CIS report.

Kansas Police Dept. Study, 1970-71
In the United States, statistics state one woman beaten every three minutes, one woman raped every seven minutes.

Australia:
'A New South Wales bricklayer shot his 56 year old de facto wife in the chest, a wound from which she died. He also attempted, but failed, to shoot her 25 year old son. On September 27th, 1973, a Central Criminal Court jury (all men) found him not guilty of murdering his de facto wife — guilty of attempted murder of the son. On the latter charge he was sentenced to 14 years jail with a non-parole period of 4 years! The judge remarked that the accused was lucky not to have killed the son and be facing a murder charge. In this case it is clear that attempting to kill another man is taken much more seriously by the judiciary than the successful killing of a woman. The total sentence, including the non-parole period, was harsher than any now being imposed for wife-killing.'
Barbara Jones, 'The Wife Killers', Vashti's Voice, June/July 1974.

New Malaysian publication on abuse of women:
The Consumer Association of Penang, Malaysia, has launched a new publication on *Abuse of Women in the Media*. The book traces how the media has been used to portray women as inferior beings and as sex objects in the areas of advertising, pornography, sex tourism, women's magazines, paperback, romances, humour, television programmes and films, and in the newspaper coverage of women. The publishers say that they believe that this is the first book from a developing country which deals with the problems of women in Malaysia and in the Third World.
IPPF, October 22, 1982.

'Every healthy vigourous male is a bottom slapper in mind if not in deed.''
Roger Gray, Q.C., Evening Standard.

That's objectionable!

Objectives:
- To consider a range of sexual harassment situations.
- To discuss and role-play possible ways of dealing with these situations.
- To practise assertive responses in dealing with sexual harassment.

Prerequisites: None.

Time needed: 50-60 minutes.

What you need: A copy of the 'That's Objectionable! situations' worksheet (p.151) and cut out each statement and paste onto a small card.

What you do:
(a) Divide the large group into small groups of 4 or 5 participants and give each group a set of the situation cards.

(b) Ask the groups to sort the cards into order with the most objectionable situation on the top of the pile and the least objectionable at the bottom.

(c) Ask each group to share their ranking and discuss any differences.

(d) Ask each group to select two situations and prepare a range of responses which they share with the group.

(e) Provide an opportunity for each participant to role play, dealing with the situations and explain the use of assertive body language in each situation (see p.19).

That's objectionable! — situations

1 The greengrocer squeezes your hand and calls you sweetheart when he gives you the change.

2 An anonymous caller breathes heavily down the phone.

3 One of the young men at work pinches your bottom as you walk past.

4 Your uncle always hugs and kisses you at family parties.

5 Your boss stands over you and stares at your breasts when you are typing.

6 A group of boys whistle as you walk past.

7 A man on the crowded bus runs his hand up your leg.

8 One of the men at work keeps telling dirty jokes and making lewd remarks.

9 Your sports teacher keeps putting his arm around you and saying what a sweet little thing you are.

10 Your boss tells you that if you are nice to him, he will give you a promotion.

11 Your male teacher keeps brushing against you and telling you that you look nice.

12 The men at work make jokes about your breasts.

Sexual harassment situations

Objectives:
- To examine different types of sexual harassment.
- To discuss the concept of appropriate and inappropriate behaviour.
- To develop strategies for dealing with sexual harassment.

Prerequisites: None.

Time needed: 45 minutes.

What you need: A set of 'Sexual harassment situation' cards for each small group. Cut out the statements and paste each on to a small card.

What you do:

(a) Divide the group into small groups of 3 or 4 and explain that each group will be given a set of the same cards.

(b) One person reads out a card in each group, and group members discuss whether they feel the behaviour described in the situation is appropriate or inappropriate. Attempt to reach consensus in the group, but if it seems to be taking too long, put the card into an 'undecided' pile and proceed.

(c) When the cards have all been finished, re-form the total group and have each small group report on which situations they found appropriate, inappropriate or undecided.

(d) Discuss the differences, and why individuals decided the way they did. Questions for general discussion could include: how do women feel and react to the kinds of situations described? Are they real? Do they happen often? Had everyone thought of them as sexual harassment before?

(e) Small groups work together to develop strategies for dealing with sexual harassment and share these with the total group.

Sexual harassment situation cards

A female school student complains to the headmaster that she is being teased by male students about the size of her breasts. The headmaster lectures her about the clothes she wears and tells her she is asking for it.	A male secretary joins the typing pool. The female secretaries joke with him about 'who he is having it off with' and make comments about his sexual prowess.
A woman walks down the road past a building site. The workers wolf whistle and call out compliments as the passes.	At a family gathering for a girl's sixteenth birthday party, she realises that her uncle has his hand on her thigh.
A woman buys a new outfit, and her next door neighbour comments on how attractive she looks the next time he sees her.	A man and woman share an office. He has pin-up photos on his wall from *Playboy* and *Penthouse*. She indicates they make her uncomfortable and asks him to take them down. He accuses her of being a prude and refuses.
The office workload is exceptionally heavy, and in order to help out the boss, who is working back until 9pm each evening, the office secretary volunteers to work back also. The next day the boss buys her flowers to say thank you.	A female student is having problems with her University course. She approaches her lecturer and he agrees to meet her and discuss her performance. At the meeting he indicates that if she will sleep with him, he will ensure that she passes.
A woman is on her way to work. The man in the flat next door comes out and says 'Oh, you have left your bra off today, you do look nice like that'. He often makes remarks about her body or appearance which she ignores.	An elderly woman is in the habit of shopping in the same grocery shop. The young male assistant starts to make comments to her, when they are alone in the store, about how beautiful she must have been when she was young, and questions about her sexual experiences.
A young woman is on a bus, it is crowded and she has to stand. Suddenly she becomes aware that the man behind her is pressing himself against her body, and he has an erection.	

Hands off

Objectives:
- To discuss the options available to young women when they are sexually harassed.
- To practise responding assertively and confidently to situations involving sexual harassment.

Prerequisites: None.

Time needed: 50-60 minutes.

What you need: A copy of 'Hands off worksheet' (p.155) for each participant.

What you do:
(a) Hand out a copy of the worksheet to each participant. Explain that this is not a test.

(b) Ask participants to form small groups, read each situation and discuss the possible responses.

(c) Ask each group to select one of the situations and prepare a role play to demonstrate the options and practise saying 'hands off'.

Variation: Ask the small group to write their own situations and role play them to the rest of the group.

'Hands off' — worksheet

How well do you cope when harassed?

Write down how you would react to the following situtations.

1 You are on your way to the shops. Walking past a quiet road you look up and realise that a man is exposing himself to you.

....

....

2 You are on a crowded bus. You become aware that the man behind you is pressing himself against you.

....

....

3 You are walking down the street. A car stops at the lights and a boy calls through the window to you saying 'Cheer up darling'.

....

....

4 A man offers you a £10 note to get into his car and go for a ride with him.

....

....

5 During a family party your uncle touches your breast.

....

....

6 A male teacher or youth leader tells you, in public, that he thinks you are very attractive.

....

....

7 You answer the telephone to hear an obscene message and heavy breathing.

....

....

8 The greengrocer holds on to your hand whilst giving you change.

....

....

Background Reading

Meulenbelt, Anja, Johanna's Daughter, *For Ourselves: Our bodies and sexuality*, Sheba Feminist Publishers, 1981.

Kitzinger, Sheila, *Woman's Experience of Sex*, Penguin, 1985.

Phillips, Angela and Rakusen, Jill, *Our Bodies Ourselves*, Penguin, 1978.

Jacobson, Bobbie, *The Ladykillers*, Pluto, 1981.

Went, Dilys, *Sex Education: Some guidelines for teachers*, Bell & Hyman, 1985.

Orbach, Suzie, *Fat is a feminist issue*, Hamlyn, 1983.

Ehrenreich, Barbara, and English, Dierdre, *For her own good: 150 years of the experts advice to women*, Pluto, 1979.

Faulder, Carolyn, *Talking to your Doctor*, Virago Handbook 2, 1975.

Macleod, Sheila, *Art of starvation*, Virago, 1981.

Farley, Lin, *Sexual Shakedown*, Melbourne House, 1978.

McConville, Bridget, *Women Under the Influence: Alcohol and its Impact*, Virago, 1983.

Graham, Hilary, *Women, Health and the Family*, Wheatsheaf Books, 1984.

Nairne, Kathy and Smith, Gerrilyn, *Dealing with Depression*, Womens Press, 1984.

Brownmiller, Susan, *Against Our Will*, Penguin, 1976.

Resources

Clarity Collective, *Taught not Caught: Strategies for sex education*, L.D.A., (British Edition 1985).

Give us a Smile. Video (13 mins). Leeds Animation Workshop, 1983.

Kenner, Charmian, *No Time for Women*. Exploring womens health in the 1930's and today. Pandora, 1985.

Body Image. Video (27 mins) made by Thames TV exploring the media images of the ideal woman. Concord Films Council Ltd., 1983.

There's More Ways Than One

Throughout our lives, we make decisions about how and where we will live, about relationships, work and what we will do with our lives. These decisions are often non-decisions: not to decide is to decide after all. In this section, we provide opportunities for women to look into the future, examine a range of options and to practise making decisions based on conscious choice. Often these choices may disagree with traditional convention, other times they will comply.

In order to challenge convention, and to achieve freedom, women need a sound knowledge of the range of options and the ability to make decisions. In this way, perhaps, we can create a world with both equal opportunities and freedom of choice for all.

Strategies

Life line interview
Fifteen years from now
I want to be like
Taking a stand
Communal living
A living space must be
I want to live in
Community child care
Time check

Decision plan
Options
Getting to know you
A relationship must be
Happy endings aren't all alike
A contract for housework
Saying no
Conflict fantasy
What would I do?

Life line interviews

Objectives:
- To commence the process of goal setting and decision making.
- To explore the reality of participant's own expectations about the future.
- To assist participants to develop confidence in approaching new people.

Prerequisites: None.

Time needed: 45-60 minutes for first session.

Time between the two sessions.

45-60 minutes for second session.

What you need: Blank pieces of paper.

What you do:

(a) Hand out blank pieces of paper with a line down the left hand side. At the top of the line, participants mark in their year of birth, further own, the present year and at the bottom the date 30 years from now.

(b) In the space between their birth and the present ask participants to write in any important life events in chronological order.

(c) Now ask them to project into the future. Think about what they will be doing over the next 30 years. Ask them to write in the significant events against the appropriate dates.

(d) In small groups, share and discuss their projected futures.

(e) Ask new small groups to form around similar projected futures, e.g. all those who will be married with children, all those who will have a career but no children, etc.

In groups of 2-3, ask them to find 3 women to interview, one 10, one 20 and one 30 years older than they are now. In the interview, they should find out what each woman is doing now, how she arrived at her present situation and how she feels about it, what she is happy about, what she regrets, etc. How do these women's lives compare to the futures projected by group members?

(f) At the next group meeting, small groups will share the outcomes of their interviews and discuss the reality of their own life line projections, and the factors they had not considered.

Variation: The participants could bring the women that they have interviewed to the next session and introduce them to the group.

Fifteen years from now . . .

Objectives:
- To provide an opportunity for participants to examine their life plans.
- To present the facts about women, work and families.

Prerequisites: For the worker to have read relevant information about women, work and the family.

Time needed: 45 minutes.

What you need: Large sheets of flipchart paper, magazines, scissors, glue, sticky tape and felt tip pens.

What you do:

(a) Ask the participants to imagine what they will be doing in 15 years. Using magazines, etc., they are to make a collage to depict this.

(b) In small groups, ask them to share and explain their collages. Ask them to make up a composite list of what they will be doing in 15 years.

(c) Share these lists in the total group and discuss the outcomes.

How many were married with children? How many were single mothers? How many had careers? How many were working? What work were they doing?

(d) Present facts about women, work and families to the group. How realistic were the members of the group about their future lives?

(e) Discuss how many of the participants plan for their futures beyond their mid 20's, and the effect this lack of planning can have on women's lives.

I want to be like . . .

Objectives:
- To develop positive female role models.
- To practise public speaking.
- To commence goal setting and decision making.

Prerequisites: This activity would be excellent at the end of a course and should follow some sessions on communication, socialization and women's role.

Time needed: 15 minutes in a previous session to explain the activity.

60-90 minutes.

What you do:

(a) In a session one or two weeks before the actual session, explain the activity to the group.

(b) Ask each participant to think of the woman from the past or present that they most want to be like. They should not tell anyone else in the group who they have chosen.

(c) Explain that on the day, they should have the following information bout her:

Date of birth;

Date of death (if appropriate);

What she achieved;

What problems she faced;

Who were the important people in her life;

Why they want to be like her;

What skills, qualities and qualifications they would need.

(d) At the actual session, provide time for each participant to present her character without providing her name.

(e) Ask the other members of the group to try to name the woman portrayed as each participant presents the facts.

(f) Provide time at the end of the session to discuss the things they learned from the activity. Ask participants to consider why they want to be like the women selected and what they would need to do to be like her.

Taking a stand

Objectives:
- To provide a structure so that a number of controversial topics can be discussed
- To provide opportunities for participants to indicate their position on a number of controversial topics.
- To introduce movement into the session.

Prerequisites: None.

Time needed: 30 minutes.

What you need: A large clear space.

5 cards at least 8" x 12" with one of the following statements printed clearly on each:

Totally unacceptable to me.

Unacceptable to me.

Don't know, not sure.

Acceptable to me.

Totally acceptable to me.

What you do:

(a) Explain to the participants that this activity provides an opportunity for them to take a stand on issues, and discuss the range of different opinions within the group.

(b) Stress that the stand taken by individuals is the one held today and that this may change as a result of discussion or further thought.

(c) Ask all of the participants to stand around the edge of the room; place the cards in a continuum along the floor.

(d) Read out one of the statements and ask participants to move quickly to the point on the continuum that best expresses their opinion on that issue at this time. Commence with non threatening or less controversial issues and move to more controversial ones.

(e) Allow participants the right to pass; this can be indicated by folded arms.

(f) When everyone has taken a stand, ask participants to form pairs and discuss the reasons why they have taken that stand. After five minutes, invite participants to share their discussions with the large group.

(g) When the major ideas have been shared, ask the group to move back and raise another issue. This process is repeated raising three, four or more issues.

Suggested issues

abortion
sex education
cigarette smoking
monogamy
communal living
divorce
women in the workplace
girls in traditionally male apprenticeships
compulsory age of consent
single sex schools
girls only clubs
equal opportunity programmes
working mothers
'kids lib'
women's liberation
in-utero fertilisation
surrogate motherhood
marijuhana smoking
polygamy
nuclear families
marriage
pre-marital sex

Communal living

Objective: ● To raise a number of issues about living with other people.

Prerequisites: None.

Time needed: 20-30 minutes.

What you need: Nothing.

What you do: (a) Explain that you will read out a statement (see suggestions below) and that people should respond quickly with hand signals, not allowing time to think too much or debate. It is to be an instant reaction and represents what a person thinks right now. Later their answer may be different.

(b) Read the statements. In this activity it is useful for the worker to participate, but delay your voting slightly so that you don't influence the group.

(c) Are you the sort of person who:

hates washing up;

likes lots of time on your own;

likes to share your bedroom;

hogs the bathroom in the morning;

wants to live with other people;

cares about your belongings;

plays the stereo really loud;

has inexpensive tastes;

is good at paying bills;

plans your dream home;

saves for the future;

(d) Ask participants to think carefully about their responses and complete one of the following sentences:

Living with me would be . . .

To live with other people I would need to . . .

A group house would . . .

(e) Ask participants to form pairs and discuss the issues involved in living with other people.

A living space must be...

Objective: ● To assist participants to set priorities about accommodation.

Prerequisites: Literacy skills.

Time needed: 35 minutes.

What you need: A copy of the 'A living space must be . . . worksheet' (p.165) for each participant.

What you do:

(a) Give each participant a copy of the worksheet.

(b) Ask them to think very carefully about their living space and what they value about it, and write one thing in each of the squares.

(c) When they have written something in each square, ask them to rank their lists in the space provided with the most important thing at the top and the least important at the bottom.

(d) Ask the participants to consider what this might express about them in terms of:

the space in which they like to live;

the people they like to live with;

the cost of accommodation;

the problems they have with accommodation.

(e) Ask each participant to complete the sentence at the bottom of their worksheet.

(f) In small groups, ask participants to share their findings.

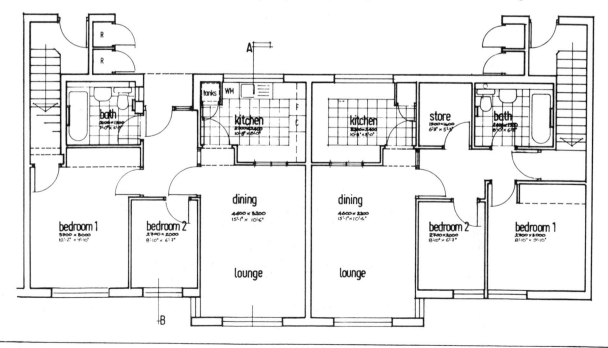

A living space must be — worksheet

<table>
<tr><td></td><td></td><td></td></tr>
<tr><td></td><td></td><td></td></tr>
<tr><td></td><td></td><td></td></tr>
</table>

Most important

1 ....

2 ....

3 ....

4 ....

5 ....

6 ....

7 ....

8 ....

9 ....

Least important

Living with me would ....

....

....

I want to live in . . .

Objectives:
- To consider the economic realities of providing accommodation for oneself and family.
- To commence setting priorities for the future.
- To explore women's economic ability to provide the accommodation of their choice.

Prerequisites: None.

Time neeeded: 50-60 minutes.

What you need: Flipchart paper, magazines, pens, glue, scissors. Copies of the 'Flats and Houses for Sale' and 'Accommodation' sections of newspapers.

What you do:
(a) Ask members of the group to make themselves comfortable and relaxed with their eyes closed.

(b) Slowly ask them to think forward into the future; to imagine themselves ten years from now.

(c) Ask them to picture:
what they look like;
what work they are doing;
who they live with
whether they have children;
where they are living.

(d) Ask them to concentrate on where they are living and imagine:
what sort of house or flat they live in;
where it is situated;
who else lives there;
what the house or flat looks like.

(e) Ask the participants to open their eyes and with the magazines and newsprint provided, make a collage to illustrate their home of the future.

(f) In small groups, compare and discuss collages.

(g) Provide each group with copies of 'Flats and Houses for Sale' and 'Accommodation' pages and ask them to cost their home of the future. Ask them to calculate both the weekly payments for their home and the percentage of the wage they will be earning in ten years, that will be spent on accommodation.

(h) In small groups, discuss whether their expectations are realistic and whether they have based their future home on being married and how they would cope if they were suddenly on their own and left with the repayments for their home.

Variation: This activity can also be done for clothes, entertainment, food, children, holidays and transport.

Community child care

Objective: ● To explore a range of child care provisions and its importance to women as workers.

Prerequisites: Discussion on women, work and the family.

Time needed: 20 minutes at the first session

Time between sessions.

60 minutes at the second session.

What you need: .Nothing.

What you do: (a) After a discussion on women, work and the family, suggest a research project to explore different kinds of child care and its importance to women as workers.

(b) Divide the group into small groups of 3-4. Each group is to contact, visit, interview and record:
a number of different child care centres (of different structures);
several working mothers who use child care;
community child care/Trades Union organisations which advocate child care.

(c) Participants in each group prepare a list of questions and observations to be made during the visits.

(d) After the visits, each small group presents their findings to the large group in whatever way they choose (e.g. role-play, street theatre, collage, guests, multi-media or audio visual presentations).

Discuss or debate the most appropriate form of child care and why child care should be provided.

Time check

Objectives:
- To provide an opportunity for participants to consider the way in which they spend their time.
- To set goals and priorities.
- To develop options for achieving goals.

Prerequisites: None.

Time needed: 30-40 minutes

What you need: A copy of the 'Time check worksheet' (p.169) for each participant.

What you do:
(a) Explain that this is a private activity and participants will only share what they choose.

(b) Hand out a copy of the worksheet to each participant and ask them to divide the first circle into sections to represent the way in which they spend their time.

(c) Ask participants to think about the differences between the way they currently spend their time and the way they would like to spend it.

(d) Using the second circle, participants allocate the amount of time that they would like to spend on the various activities in their lives and then complete the two sentence stems.

(e) In small groups, ask participants to discuss the ways in which their time can be re-allocated and used to achieve different goals.

Time check — worksheet

The way I spend my time:

I spend most of my time on ....

....

....

The way I want to use my time:

I would like to change ....

....

....

about the way I spend my time.

To do this I will ....

....

Decision plan

Objective: ● To develop the skills of decision making.

Prerequisites: For the worker: to have read the section on Decision Making (p.22).

Time needed: 30 minutes.

What you need: Flipchart paper and felt tip pens.

What you do:

(a) Identify a particular issue which poses a problem. For example: a woman has two young children and needs to find work. How will she decide on child care? Whatever the issue, break it down to its basic elements, consider these until they can be visualised as two possibilities.

(b) At the top of a sheet of flipchart paper, or whiteboard, write the problem. By discussing the options and their possible outcomes develop a plan (see pages 22-23).

(c) At each stage of developing the plan, it is important to discuss what the alternatives are; what will be missed by opting for one possible alternative and not the others? As the plan grows, the decisions become more complex. Concentrate on action; what can be done and what will be the result?

(d) When all the options have been generated and discussed, order the range of options into priority; which is the best choice?

(e) Discuss how this procedure can be used by individuals in solving their own problems and point out that, by using the technique, people can develop a range of options, and how making a particular choice can have long term implications.

Note: This strategy can be used by individuals when faced with a personal dilemma, or a problem in the community. When solving a more complex problem, it may be necessary to develop the plan over a longer period, allowing time to research the answers to questions the group does not understand.

Options

Objectives:
- To explore options in specific situations.
- To practise decision making skills.

Prerequisites: For the worker: to have read the sections on 'Decision Making' and 'Priority Setting' (pp.22-24).

Time needed: 45 minutes.

What you need: A copy (or copies) of the 'Option worksheet' (p.172) for each participant. A copy of the 'options chart' on a large board or flipchart paper.

What you do:

(a) Explain to the group that there are usually a number of options or solutions for each situation or problem and that this strategy will help to develop skills in decision making.

(b) Read one of the situation stories (p.173) and ask participants to call out the options that are available to the person in the story. Write this in the 'options' column on the board.

(c) Ask participants to specify the disadvantages, advantages and possible outcome for each option.

(d) Let participants practise two or three situations.

(e) In small groups, ask participants to develop some problem situations from their own experience, and then use the worksheet to explore the options and make decisions.

Options — worksheet

Problem or goal ....

....

Options	Disadvantages	Advantages	Possible outcome

Priority listing of options

1 ....

2 ....

3 ....

4 ....

5 ....

The best course of action is ....

....

....

Because ....

....

....

....

....

Options situations

Swimming

You go swimming with a group of friends who are more experienced than you. You have had some beginners' lessons and need more. Your friends tell you that all you need is practice and that they will look after you. What do you do?

Smoking

You are offered a cigarette by a girl who you would really like to be friends with. She laughs when you tell her you've never smoked. Will you take a cigarette?

Sam's story

Sam has been married for ten years and has three children. Before she was married, she worked as a primary school teacher. Now her husband wants a divorce. He plans to sell the house and move to another town. Sam will need to support herself and the children with some assistance from her husband. What should Sam do?

Jesse's story

Jesse has always wanted to be an actress but her family do not want her to go to drama school. She is very good with her hands and they want her to learn a trade so that she will have a secure job. What should she do?

Angela's and Hannah's story

Angela has missed the last train home and she and her friend Hannah are offered a lift home by some people they know. The driver has had too much to drink. What will Angela do? What will Hannah do?

Jenny's story

Jenny is very happy in her job and is proficient and reliable. Her boss often praises her work but has never mentioned a promotion or a pay increase. Jenny is starting to feel angry about her situation. What should she do to get the increase or promotion that she thinks she deserves?

Getting to know you

Objectives: ● To explore a range of different life styles.

                   ● To examine attitudes to different lifestyles.

Prerequisites: Some involvement in role play.

                   For the worker — To have read the section on Role Play (p.27).

Time needed: 60 minutes.

What you need: A set of the Role Statements. If the group is larger, add some extra roles or appoint observers.

What you do:

(a) Hand out one Role Statement to each participant, and explain that each person will be playing the role of the character written on their statement.

(b) Ask each participant to choose a name which she will use for the role play; suggest that the name be consistent with the character she is to play.

(c) Set the scene for the role play by explaining to the group that for the purpose of this activity they are all going on a safari. The week before they are due to leave, they will attend a briefing meeting with the safari leader. On arrival at her office they find a note to say that the leader is ill and that the meeting is postponed. It is suggested by one of the characters that, as everyone is present, they could go to the local pub, have a drink and get to know each other.

(d) Commence the role play. Ensure that each participant remains in character and allow the role play to continue for 20-30 minutes.

(e) When the time is up, de-role the characters. Ask the observers to join the group and report their observations.

(f) Focus discussion on the range of lifestyles represented, the way in which characters interacted and the attitudes expressed during the role play. Explore the myths and reality of the assumptions made by group members about people with lifestyles different from their own.

Variation: Towering Inferno

(a) Hand out the list of characters to each participant.

(b) Explain that all of the characters are together on the 10th floor of a building when a fire starts. Only one fire ladder is available for escape.

(c) Ask each participant to rank the order in which the characters should leave the building.

(d) Form the group into small groups of five or six and ask them to reach consensus on the ranking.

(e) Share the rankings in the large group and explore the attitudes and assumptions expressed.

Getting to know you — role statements

A career woman, violinist, no children by choice, happily married, Italian, living in inner-city terraced house.	A single father, civil servant, an Indian, teenage son and daughter, living in inner city house.
A gay man living in suburban home with 3 other people; successful surgeon.	A young man from the country just finished apprenticeship, looking for work, lives in a hostel.
Lesbian mother of 2, director of community health centre, lives in a country town with her mother and children.	A grandmother bringing up her son's two children, never been in paid employment, dedicated community volunteer.
Single heterosexual woman carpenter, born in America, lives in a caravan.	Single mother of one young child, struggling artist, lives in a flat above a bookshop.
Unemployed marketing manager, male, married, 3 children, lives in a suburban house, wife is dental assistant.	West Indian man, happily married, lecturer in political science and writer, no children, lives in a university college.
Woman, dental assistant, married, 3 children, lives in suburban house, husband an unemployed marketing manager.	Women's sports instructress. Spends half the year abroad.
Feminist philosopher and writer, widow, mother of two adult daughters, lives in a communal household.	Long distance lorry driver, West Indian, widower, one young child, lives in Black area of a big city.

A relationship must be . . .

Objectives:
- To examine priorities within relationships.
- To commence priority setting about relationships.

Prerequisites: None.

Time needed: 45-50 minutes.

What you need: A pen and Copy of 'A relationship must be . . .' worksheet (p.178) for each participant.

What you do:
(a) Ask each participant to think carefully about what they most want from a relationship and then write their requirements in the eight spaces provided on the worksheet.

(b) When they have finished, ask them to order their requirements on the scale provided, from the most important to the least important.

(c) Ask participants to complete the three sentences at the bottom of the page.

(d) In small groups discuss their priorities and expectations in relationships. What is the difference in relationships? What is the difference between what they want from a relationship with the same sex and the opposite sex?

A relationship must be . . . worksheet

Most important:

1 ....

2 ....

3 ....

4 ....

5 ....

6 ....

7 ....

8 ....

Least important:

For me, a relationship must be: ....

....

With a member of the same sex, a relationship must be ....

....

With a member of the opposite sex, a relationship must be: ....

....

....

Happy endings aren't all alike

Objectives:	• To examine sex role expectations as they relate to career choices for women and men.
	• To introduce a range of life style options.
Prerequisites:	Literacy skills.
Time needed:	45 minutes.
What you need:	A copy of the 'Happy endings' story (p.180) for each participant.
What you do:	(a) Hand out a copy of the story to each participant

(b) Ask them to read the story without discussing it and then to write an ending for the story.

(c) In small groups, ask the participants to share their endings.

(d) Ask the small groups to share their endings and write the major points on a white board or flipchart paper. Add any of the possible endings (see below) that have not already been listed.

(e) Ask the small groups to reverse the story so that it is Jo who is offered the promotion and then consider which ending they would use. If there is a difference, ask them to consider why it is different.

(f) In the large group discuss:
the conditions necessary for each of the endings to occur;
the long term outcomes of the endings;
the endings that the participants would prefer for themselves.

Happy endings — possible endings

1 Jo leaves her job and goes to Manchester with Sam and quickly finds a new exciting job.
2 Sam doesn't take the promotion and stays in London. Two months later, another promotion becomes available.
3 Jo and Sam both leave their jobs and move to a new town.
4 Sam moves to Manchester and Jo stays in London and they see each other once a fortnight for four days and on holidays, and talk to each other on the phone every day.
5 Jo goes to Manchester with Sam and can't find a new job.
6 Jo and Sam agree that if Jo can't find a job in Manchester within three months, they will return to London. Jo takes unpaid leave and goes to Manchester.
7 Jo and Sam decide to go the Manchester. They agree that it is a good time for them to have a baby. Jo arranges two years' leave without pay from her job.
8 Sam doesn't take the promotion and stays in London.

Happy Endings — Story

Jo had just finished tidying her desk. She looked at her watch, it was six o'clock. Her secretary had already left but Jo had another hour's work in front of her. She smiled, her new job was exciting and a challenge and she knew that she was coping and doing it well. She thought of Sam as she gazed out of the window into the London twilight.

He would be arriving home by now and deciding what they would have for supper. Their new home, close to his office, was ideal; he could arrive home early and get a meal ready. The telephone rang.

'It's Sam, I've worked a little late so I thought we'd eat out tonight. And anyway, there's some things I need to discuss with you.'

'Sounds fine, I'll see you at Mario's at eight.'

'Great. See you there.'

Sam was already at the table when Jo arrived at the restaurant. She could tell from his grin that he had something important to tell her.

'O.K., Sam, I can tell you can't wait. What is it, love?'

'Well, it's the promotion we've both been hoping for. I've got it. The Boss offered me a new position today!'

'Oh, how wonderful! How marvellous! We must celebrate. Let's have champagne!'

'Jo . . .'

'Waiter! Sam, I'm so pleased for you! Oh, waiter, champagne, please, the best you've got!'

'Jo . . .'

'Darling Sam, you deserve it, it's . . .'

'Jo! Please. You don't understand, I haven't finished. The position, the position I've been offered? It's in Manchester, we'll have to move.'

'Move? Sam, move? You, you can't be serious? You're going to take a job that means leaving this city — when I've just had the chance of a lifetime in my own career?'

Their eyes met across the table, two strong people, in love and not reaching each other. The waiter arrived and poured their champagne.

'Jo, what are we going to do?'

A contract for housework

Objectives:
- To explore roles and expectations about housework.
- To develop a contract for housework
- To develop skills of negotiating.

Prerequisites: None.

Time needed: 60 minutes.

What you need: Nothing.

What you do:
(a) Ask participants to work in small groups of 4-0, ask each group to appoint a recorder.

(b) Each small group is to discuss and develop a contract for housework, covering responsibility for tasks, frequency, duration, who is responsible (where applicable), etc.

(c) When complete, each group shares their contract, discusses and amends them until there is consensus about a contract for the entire group.

(d) Ask the group to form pairs or small groups of up to 6 people, and each group to prepare a role play (p.27) in which they negotiate responsibility for housework, using the contract as a guide. They should decide on what other roles and responsibilities each person in the situation carries (do they work full or part-time? are there children? how many? what ages are they? and take these into account in their role play.

(e) Groups then present their role plays.

(f) After de-roling and de-briefing (p.28), discuss the different role plays, and highlight any useful points, discuss any that may seem unhelpful.

(g) Discuss the concept of negotiating housework, and whether the group members will use the contract in future situations.

Saying no

Objectives:
- To provide participants with practise in making simple requests.
- To consider and practise a number of ways of saying no.
- To examine the feelings associated with saying no.

Prerequisites: Group members need some knowledge of each other.

Time needed: 45-60 minutes.

What you need: Large room so that the groups can work without disturbing each other. Small note pads and pens for each participant. Flipchart paper and felt tip pens.

What you do:

(a) Divide the large group into pairs of groups with 5-7 members in each. Identify which pairs of groups will be working together and ensure that each person knows the names of the members of their paired group.

(b) Explain to the groups that each person is going to make a request for something from each of the members of their paired group. In deciding what to request, suggest that they be realistic and creative. For example, they may ask to borrow something; for help with some work; to do something together.

(c) When each of the participants has completed writing their requests, they communicate these to the members of their paired group and hand each person the slip of paper with the request written on it as a reminder. At this stage those receiving requests should not give any answer, but defer until later.

To: *(name of member(s) of paired group)*

Request: *(written here)*

From:

(d) When all of the requests have been exchanged, participants should return to their group. Ask each group to list on flipchart paper all the possible ways of saying 'no'; consider what the likely effect(s) of these might be; discuss the most appropriate ways of saying 'no'.

(e) Explain that participants are going to say 'no' to all of the requests no matter how difficult it may be. Ask them to decide, taking into consideration the previous discussions, how they will do it.

(g) When they have finished, the paired groups, meet together and discuss how individuals felt about saying 'no': were some requests harder to refuse than others? What made the difference? Accepting no — were the refusals reasonable? Was it harder to hear 'no' from some people than it was from others? What was the difference?

The small groups keep a record of these discussions on flip charts to share with the total group.

(h) In the total group, discuss the ways the groups considered to say 'no' and how these might be accepted?

Do women find it harder to say 'no' than men?

Why might that be?

What are the situations in which participants find it most difficult to say 'no'? Are there common factors?

Conflict fantasy

Objectives: ● To consider the ways in which we deal with conflict.

● To practise appropriate conflict resolution behaviour.

Prerequisites: A discussion of conflict and methods of dealing with it (p.21).

Time needed: 45-60 minutes.

What you need: A white board or large sheet of flipchart paper.

What you do: (a) Ask participants to sit in a relaxed comfortable position and close their eyes.

(b) Ask each individual to imagine that they are walking down a long tunnel or passage. A long way ahead they can see someone coming towards them. While the person is still a long way off they realise that it is someone with whom they are having an argument or disagreement.

(c) Ask each person to think about what they will do. What are the options and which one will they choose?

(d) Form small groups of 3-4 participants and ask each group to generate a list of options and discuss the relative merits of each option.

(e) Ask everyone to close their eyes again and imagine that they are getting closer to the person and will have to take some action. What is it? How do they feel about the action? Would they like to change it?

(f) Ask the large group to place the options on a continuum and comment on the productive/non-productive options (see p.21).

Note: If the individuals are willing, some of the fantasies could be role played; relate to assertive behaviour and self confidence.

What would I do?

Objectives:
- To identify the difference between passive, assertive and aggressive behaviour.
- To consider a range of responses to specified situations.
- To practise assertive ways of responding in situations.

Prerequisites: None.

Time needed: 50-60 minutes.

What you need: A pen and a copy of the 'What would I do? worksheet' (p.186) for each participant.

What you do:

(a) Hand out a copy of the worksheet to each participant and ask them to complete it independantly.

(b) Divide the group into small groups of 3-4 to discuss the individual responses and to come to agreement on which behaviour is assertive, passive or aggressive.

(c) Hand out copies of the 'practise sheet' and ask each small group to develop their own responses.

(d) Ask each group to select one or two examples from the list and prepare a role play to demonstrate the different responses.

(e) Ask each group to present their role play to the large group and discuss what factors verbal and non-verbal, made the difference between assertive, passive and aggressive behaviour.

(f) Provide opportunities for all members of the group to practise responding assertively to the range of situations.

Follow up: Ask participants to prepare and practice assertive responses to situations from their own experience.

'What would I do? — worksheet

Rank the following choices 1, 2, 3. '1' is the action you would often take:

1 Your parents have just criticised your partner/boyfriend/girlfriend. You feel the criticism is unfair and say:
   a. Shut up. You're both stupid.
   b. I guess you're right.
   c. I feel that you are being unfair. She/he isn't like that.

2 You are with a group of friends and deciding which film to see. One person has suggested one that you don't want to see. You say:
   a. I don't want to see that film. What about seeing . . .?
   b. You always choose, can't someone else have a turn?
   c. I guess so. I don't really mind.

3 A friend is talking on and on and you need to get home. You say:
   a. You know I have to be home by five. Now you've made me late.
   b. Nothing. Just keep listening.
   c. I really have to go. I'm expected home at 5.00.

4 A friend has just said your jacket looks good. It's a new one and you like it. You say:
   a. Thank you.
   b. Oh this, it's okay, I suppose.
   c. Why did you say that?

5 New people have moved across the road and you would like to meet them. You:
   a. Smile when you see them.
   b. Watch through the window and try to be outside when you see them coming.
   c. Go over and introduce yourself.

6 You ordered a coke and hamburger well done. The coke is warm and the hamburger is rare. You say:
   a. I would like a cold coke please and my hamburger is not how I ordered it.
   b. It's fine, it doesn't matter.
   c. This just isn't good enough. I'm not coming here again.

7 A friend was to pick you up at home. She/he is one hour late. When they arrive you say:
   a. About time. What do you think this is?
   b. Hi, how are you?
   c. I was worried. I would have liked you to phone and say you would be late.

8 You buy a new pair of jeans and when you get home find a button is missing. You:
   a. Do nothing and wear them anyway.
   b. Return them to the shop and ask for an exchange or refund.
   c. Leave them in the cupboard and refuse to wear them.

'What Would I Do?' practice sheet

Now You Practice. Think of ways you could react in the following situations:

9 You want to do a mechanics course and your friends are teasing you.
10 You have been standing in a queue for ages and someone pushes in front of you.
11 Your boyfriend wants you to stay overnight when his parents are away and you don't want to.
12 Your sister is using the phone and you want to make an important call.
13 Your teacher makes a mistake in marking your exam paper.

Background Reading

Gavron, Hannah, *The Captive Wife*, Penguin, 1966.
Bailey, Caro, *A Loving Conspiracy: Marriage in the 1980's*, Quartet, 1984.
Oakley, Ann, *Sex, Gender and Family*, Temple Smith, 1972.
Oakley, Ann, *Housewife*, Penguin, 1977.

Resources

Adams, Carol and Laurikietis, Rae, *The Gender Trap — Sex and Marriage*, Virago, 1976.
Lifeskills Associates, *Lifeskills Teaching Programme No.1*, 1979, *Lifeskills Teaching Programme No.2*, 1982, Lifeskills Associates.
Eisenstadt, N. and Braun, D. *What is a Family?* Community Education Development Centre, 1985.
Living Choice, CRAC Publications, 1976.
Maidenhead Teachers' Centre, *Doing Things In and About the Home*, Serawood House (Publishers) Ltd., 1983.
Braun, D. and Eisenstadt, N. *Family Lifestyles*, Open University Press, 1985.
Framed Youth. Video (50 mins) in which young lesbian and gay people talk about their lives. Albany Video, 1983.

Strategy Index

Useful Addresses

ALBANY VIDEO
The Albany
Douglas Way
London SE8 4AG
Tel: 01-692 6322

A WOMAN'S PLACE
Hungerford House
Victoria Embankment
London WC2
Tel: 01-836 6081

BLACK WOMEN'S CENTRE
41 Stockwell Green
London SW9
Tel: 01-274 9220

BFI PUBLICATIONS
81 Dean Street
London W1

BRITISH PREGNANCY ADVISORY
SERVICE (BPAS)
Second Floor
58 Petty France
London SW1 Tel: 01-222 0985

BROOK ADVISORY CENTRES
Education and Publications Unit
10 Albert Street
Birmingham B4 7UD
Tel: 021-643 1554

CAMBRIDGE WOMEN'S RESOURCES
CENTRE
7C Station Road
Cambridge CB1 2JB
Tel: (0223) 321148

CARDIFF WOMEN'S CENTRE
2 Coburn Strreet
Cathays, Cardiff
Tel: (0222) 374051

CFL VISION
Chalfont Grove
Gerrards Cross
Bucks. SL9 8TN
Tel: 02407 4433

CINEMA OF WOMEN
27 Clerkenwell Close
London EC1R 0AT
Tel: 01-251 4978

CONCORD FILMS COUNCIL LTD
201 Felixstowe Road
Ipswich IP3 9BJ
Tel: 0473 715754

CONNEXIONS
4th Floor
18-20 Dean Street
NEwcastle-upon-Tyne NE1 1PG

CROMER STREET WOMEN'S CENTRE
90 Cromer Street
London WC1
Tel: 01-278 0120

CURRICULUM DEVELOPMENT SUPPORT
UNIT
Donnington Road
London NW10 3JG

EQUAL OPPORTUNITIES COMMISSION
(EOC)
Quay Street
Manchester 33HN
Tel: 061-833 9244

FAMILY PLANNING ASSOCIATION
27-35 Mortimer Street
London W1N 7RJ
Tel:01-636 7866

FAWCETT LIBRARY
City of London Polytechnic
Old Castle Street
London E1 7NT
Tel: 01-283 1030

FEMINIST ARCHIVE
Bath University
Claverton Down
Bath BA2 7AY
Tel: (0225) 312703

FEMINIST BOOK FAIR GROUP
Room 306
38 Mount Pleasant
London WC1
Tel: 01-837 9666

FEMINIST HISTORY GROUP
c/o Mary Ward Centre
Queens Square
London WC1
Tel: 01-493 8131

FEMINIST LIBRARY AND INFORMATION
CENTRE
Hungerford House
Victoria Embankment
London WC2N 6PA
Tel: 01-930 0715

FORMAT PHOTOGRAPHERS
25 Horsell Road
London N5
Tel: 01-609 3439

GLASGOW WOMEN'S CENTRE
57 Millar Street
Glasgow
Tel: (041) 2211177

GUILD SOUND AND VISION
6 Royce Road
Peterborough PE1 5YB
Tel: (0733) 315315

HEALTH EDUCATION AUTHORITY (HEA)
Hamilton House
Mabledon Place
London WC1H 9TX

ILEA PUBLISHING CENTRE
Thackeray Road
London SW8 3TB
Tel: 01-622 9966

LEEDS ANIMATION WORKSHOP
45 Bayswater Row
Leeds
W. Yorks. LS8 5LF
Tel: (0532) 484997

LESBIAN LINE
BM Box 1514
London WC1N 3XX
Tel: 01-251 6911

LESBIAN LINK
62 Bloom Street
Manchester
Tel: 061-236 6205

LIFESKILLS ASSOCIATES
Ashling
Backchurch Lane
Leeds LS16 8DN
Tel: 0532 741000

LONDON LESBIAN LINE
52 Featherstone Street
London EC1
Tel: 01-251 6911

LONDON RAPE CRISIS CENTRE
PO Box 69
London WC1X 9NJ
Tel: 01-837 1600 (rape crisis)
        01-278 3956 (other information)

LONDON WOMEN'S AID
52-54 Featherstone Street
London EC1
Tel: 01-251 6537

MICROSYSTER
Wesley House
Wild Court
London WC2
Tel: 01-430 0655

NATIONAL ABORTION CAMPAIGN
75 Kingsway
London WC2
Tel: 01-993 2071/405 4801

NATIONAL ADVISORY CENTRE ON
CAREERS FOR WOMEN (NACCW)
Drayton House
30 Gordon Street
London WC1H 0AX
Tel: 01-380 0117

NATIONAL YOUTH BUREAU
17-23 Albion Street
Leicester LE1 6GD
Tel: (0533) 554775

NOTHERN IRELAND WOMEN IN
EDUCATION
17 Ardmore Avenue
Ballyateign
Belfast 7
Tel: (0232) 646530

NORTHERN IRELAND ASSOCIATION OF
YOUTH CLUBS
Hampton
Glenmachan Park
Belfast 4

OASIS PUBLICATIONS
Cherry Tree House
Newton-on-Ouse
York Y06 2BN

OTHER CINEMA
79 Wardour Street
London W1V 3TH
Tel: 01-734 8508

PREGNANCY ADVISORY SERVICE
11-13 Charlotte Street
London W1
Tel: 01-637 8962

RESOURCES & INFORMATION FOR GIRLS
25 Bayham Street
London NW1
Tel: 01-387 7450

RIGHTS OF WOMEN
52-54 Featherstone Street
London EC1
Tel: 01-251 6577

SEE RED WOMEN'S WORKSHOP
16A Iliffe Yard
London SE17
Tel: 01-701 8314

SHEBA FEMINIST PUBLISHERS
488 Kingsland Road
London E8 4AE
Tel: 01-254 1590

SHEFFIELD WOMEN & EDUCATION
GROUP
29 Parkers Road
Sheffield S10 1BN
Tel: (0742) 664862

SISTERS AGAINST DISABLEMENT
241 Albion Road
London N16
Tel: 01-241 2263

SIZE 8 COLLECTIVE
Abraham Moss Centre
Crescent Road
Manchester M8 6UF
Tel: 061-740 1491

SPARE TYRE
86-88 Holmleigh Road
London N16
Tel: 01-809 1040

THE WOMEN'S PRESS LTD
34 Great Sutton Street
London EC1 0DX
Tel: 01-251 3007

TUC WOMEN'S ADVISORY COMMITTEE
Congress House
23 Great Russell Street
London WC1B 3LF
Tel: 01-636 4030

WOMEN AND MANUAL TRADES
52 Featherstone Street
London EC1
Tel: 01-251 9192/3

WOMEN AND WORK HAZARDS GROUP
9 Poland Street
London W1
Tel: 01-437 2728

WOMEN'S EDUCATION GROUP
Women's Education Resource Centre
ILEA Drama and Tape Centre
Princeton Street
London WC1

WOMEN'S ARCHIVE AND LIBRARY
PROJECT, OXFORD (WALPO)
Wholemeal
Cowley Road
Oxford
Tel: (0865) 54150

WOMEN'S EDUCATIONAL ADVISORY
COMMITTEE (WEAC)
Worker's Educational Association National
Office
9 Upper Berkeley Street
London W1H 8BY
Tel: 01-402 5608

WOMEN'S INFORMATION REFERRAL
AND ENQUIRY SERVICE (WIRES)
PO Box 162
Sheffield 1 1UD
Tel: (0742) 755290

WOMEN IN MEDIA
Box BM-WIM
London WC1N 3XX
Tel: 01-380 0517

WOMEN'S COMPUTER CENTRE
Wesley House
Wild Court
London WC2
Tel: 01-430 0112

WOMEN'S HEALTH INFORMATION
CENTRE
52-54 Featherstone Street
London EC1
Tel: 01-251 6589

WOMEN'S NATIONAL COMMISSION
Government Offices
Great George Street
London SW1P 3AQ
Tel: 01-233 4208

WOMEN'S THERAPY CENTRE
6 Manor Gardens
London N7 6LA
Tel: 01-263 6200

VIRAGO PRESS LTD
41 William IVth Street
London WC2
Tel: 01-379 6977

YWCA
Hampden House
2 Weymouth Street
London W1N 4AX
Tel: 01-631 0657